Get the most from this book

Everyone has to decide his or her own revision strategy, but it is essential to review your work, learn it and test your understanding. These Revision Notes will help you do that in a planned way, topic by topic. They cover the two Ethics modules (RSS01 and RSS02) and the two Philosophy of Religion modules (RSS03 and RSS04). Use this book as the cornerstone of your revision and don't hesitate to write in it – personalise your notes and check your progress by ticking off each section as you revise.

☑ **Tick to track your progress**

Use the revision planner on pages 4 and 5 to plan your revision, topic by topic. Tick each box when you have:

● revised and understood a topic
● tested yourself
● practised the exam questions and gone online to check your answers.

You can also keep track of your revision by ticking off each topic heading in the book. You may find it helpful to add your own notes as you work through each topic.

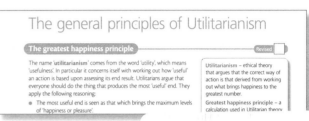

Features to help you succeed

Exam tips

Throughout the book there are tips to help you boost your final grade.

Typical mistakes

Identifies the typical mistakes candidates make.

Now test yourself

These short, knowledge-based questions provide the first step in testing your learning. Check your answers at www.therevisionbutton.co.uk/myrevisionnotes

Key words

Clear, concise definitions of essential key terms are provided on the page where they appear.

Key quotes

Quotations from key scholars concisely express key ideas or views relevant to each topic.

Exam practice

Practice exam questions are provided for each topic. Use them to consolidate your revision and practise your exam skills.

Online

Go online to check your answers to the exam questions and the Now test yourself questions and try out the extra quick quizzes at www.therevisionbutton.co.uk/myrevisionnotes

My revision planner

Exam practice answers at **www.therevisionbutton.co.uk/myrevisionnotes**

Unit D Religion, Philosophy and Science

	Revised	Tested	Exam ready
4.1 Miracles			
113 A miracle as a violation of Natural Law	☐	☐	☐
117 A miracle as an event of religious significance	☐	☐	☐
119 Issues arising	☐	☐	☐
4.2 Creation			
121 Religious beliefs about the creation of the world	☐	☐	☐
123 God and the created world	☐	☐	☐
124 Scientific theories about the nature, origin and end of the universe	☐	☐	☐
127 Scientific theory about the origin and development of life	☐	☐	☐
128 Issues arising	☐	☐	☐
4.3 The design argument			
131 Forms of the argument	☐	☐	☐
133 Key criticisms of the design argument	☐	☐	☐
136 Issues arising	☐	☐	☐
4.4 Quantum mechanics and a religious world view			
137 Challenges to Newtonian physics	☐	☐	☐
138 Key ideas in the world view of quantum mechanics	☐	☐	☐
141 Quantum mechanics and religion	☐	☐	☐
143 Issues arising	☐	☐	☐

Assessment Objectives (AO)

For AS Religious Studies you must sit *two* modules. Each module has four questions of which you must answer any two. Each question is divided into two parts. The first part assesses the Assessment Objective knowledge and understanding. The second part of the question assesses the Assessment Objective evaluation. It is therefore important to be aware of the weighting for each Assessment Objective in each module.

Assessment Objective			For each question	Module weighting
AO1	Knowledge and understanding	Select and demonstrate clearly relevant knowledge and understanding through the use of evidence, examples and correct language and terminology appropriate to the course of study.	30 marks	66.7%
AO2	Evaluation	Critically evaluate and justify a point of view through the use of evidence and reasoned argument.	15 marks	33.3%

Countdown to my exams

6–8 weeks to go

- Start by looking at the specification available from www.aqa.org.uk. Make sure you know exactly what material you need to revise and the style of the examination. Use the revision planner on pages 4 and 5 to familiarise yourself with the topics.

- Organise your notes, making sure you have covered everything on the specification. The revision planner will help you group your notes into topics.

- Work out a realistic revision plan that will allow you time for relaxation. Set aside days and times for all the subjects that you need to study, and stick to your timetable.

- Set yourself sensible targets. Break your revision down into focused sessions of around 40 minutes, divided by breaks. These Revision Notes organise the basic facts into short, memorable sections to make revising easier.

Revised ☐

4–6 weeks to go

- Read through the relevant sections of this book and refer to the examiner's tips, typical mistakes and key terms. Tick off the topics as you feel confident about them. Highlight those topics you find difficult and look at them again in detail.

- Test your understanding of each topic by working through the 'Now test yourself' questions in the book. Look up the answers at www.therevisionbutton.co.uk/myrevisionnotes

- Make a note of any problem areas as you revise, and ask your teacher to go over these in class.

- Look at past papers. They are one of the best ways to revise and practise your exam skills. Write or prepare planned answers to the exam practice questions provided in this book. Check your answers online and try out the extra quick quizzes at www.therevisionbutton.co.uk/myrevisionnotes

- Try different revision methods. For example, you can make notes using mind maps, spider diagrams or flash cards.

- Track your progress using the revision planner and give yourself a reward when you have achieved your target.

Revised ☐

One week to go

- Try to fit in at least one more timed practice of an entire past paper and seek feedback from your teacher, comparing your work closely with the mark scheme.

- Check the revision planner to make sure you haven't missed out any topics. Brush up on any areas of difficulty by talking them over with a friend or getting help from your teacher.

- Attend any revision classes put on by your teacher. Remember, he or she is an expert at preparing people for examinations.

Revised ☐

The day before the examination

- Flick through these Revision Notes for useful reminders, for example the examiner's tips, typical mistakes and key words.

- Check the time and place of your examination.

- Make sure you have everything you need – extra pens and pencils, tissues, a watch, bottled water, sweets.

- Allow some time to relax and have an early night to ensure you are fresh and alert for the examinations.

Revised ☐

My exams

AS Religion and Ethics 1 – RSS01

Date: ....

Time: ....

Location: ....

AS Religion and Ethics 2 – RSS02

Date: ....

Time: ....

Location: ....

AS Philosophy of Religion – RSS03

Date: ....

Time: ....

Location: ....

AS Religion, Philosophy and Science – RSS04

Date: ....

Time: ....

Location: ....

1.1 Utilitarianism

The general principles of Utilitarianism

The greatest happiness principle Revised

The name '**utilitarianism**' comes from the word 'utility', which means 'usefulness'. In particular it concerns itself with working out how 'useful' an action is based upon assessing its end result. Utilitarians argue that everyone should do the thing that produces the most 'useful' end. They apply the following reasoning:

- The most useful end is seen as that which brings the maximum levels of 'happiness or pleasure'.
- Therefore actions that produce the most happiness are seen as the best course of action (i.e. good moral actions).
- This way of assessing which course of action is the best one to take is known as 'the **greatest happiness principle**'.

Since utilitarianism is concerned about the outcome (or 'end') of an action, it is a **teleological** ethical theory.

> **Utilitarianism** – ethical theory that argues that the correct way of action is that derived from working out what brings happiness to the greatest number.
>
> **Greatest happiness principle** – a calculation used in Utilitarian theory to assess the best course of action to take.
>
> **Teleological** – an ethical theory that considers the consequences of a particular action, or the 'end' result, and it is the assessment of this 'end' that determines whether or not the action is morally good.

Typical mistake

Make sure that you have a good grasp of key words and technical terminology. It is important to know what they mean and to use them correctly. Mistakes are made in examinations when candidates confuse terms or just get them wrong to the detriment of the overall level achieved.

Now test yourself

1 Explain the term 'Utilitarianism'.
2 What is the 'greatest happiness principle'?

Answers online

Tested

Deontological thinking in contrast to consequential or teleological thinking Revised

Deontological thinking

Deontological ethical theories are concerned with the acts themselves, irrespective of the consequences of those acts. For example, a deontologist might reason:

- to take away life is wrong irrespective of the situation or consequence
- therefore euthanasia is morally wrong.

Deontological systems have been criticised as being too intolerant by coldly calculating a moral judgement irrespective of individual circumstances. In addition, such thinking can be offensive towards different cultures or ideologies. It implies that only one view is correct and therefore all other views are in error. As Simon Blackburn, professor of

> **Deontological** – a term used to denote an ethical theory that is based upon the belief that an action is intrinsically wrong or right, irrespective of consequences.

philosophy, writes: 'Nobody is comfortable now with the blanket colonial certainty that just our way of doing things is right, and that other people need forcing into those ways.'

Consequential or teleological thinking

The word 'teleological' comes from the Greek meaning 'end' or 'purpose'. Teleological thinking considers the consequences of a particular action or the 'end' result, and it is the assessment of this 'end' that determines whether or not the action is morally good. As it considers consequences it is also known as 'consequential thinking'. In the case of Utilitarianism, the theory holds that the action that best results in 'the greatest happiness for the greatest number' is the right action.

Now test yourself

3   What is consequential thinking?

Answer online

Tested

Bentham's Utilitarianism

Jeremy Bentham

Revised

Jeremy Bentham (1748–1832) is usually accepted as the thinker who developed Utilitarianism as a systematic theory. He was a social reformer and sought to develop an ethical theory which promoted actions that would benefit the majority of people. For him, happiness was the supreme ethical value, or what he called the 'sovereign good'. Happiness is useful, because it is good for people to be happy. Bentham argued that we are motivated by pleasure and pain and that we pursue pleasure and avoid pain. This view of happiness being linked to pleasure owes something to an earlier ethical theory called hedonism. In hedonism, the only thing that is right is pleasure.

Greatest happiness (for the greatest number)

Although Utilitarianism is a teleological ethical theory, there is a rule or guiding principle underpinning this approach. This guiding principle is known as the principle of utility, and states that people should act to bring about the greatest happiness for the greatest number.

However, there is danger in interpreting what this means in practice as it is a slightly misleading summary of the principle at face value. This is because the greatest happiness does not necessarily involve the greatest number of people. Rather, the emphasis is more on the action that produces the greatest amount of happiness overall. In other words, what maximises happiness is what is right.

> **Typical mistake**
>
> When answering a question, remain focused on the title of the question. Often candidates are drawn into digression by writing biographical details or information that is not directly relevant to the focus of the question, e.g. some interesting information about Jeremy Bentham's childhood.

The hedonic calculus

Revised

Having established that the measure of happiness is the criterion for a right act, there arises the problem of how to calculate that measurement. For Bentham, happiness consists of pleasure minus pain. The principle of utility, or usefulness, centres on the act delivering the greatest amount of pleasure and the least amount of pain. Bentham's solution to measuring this balance was his '**hedonic calculus**'. Other names for it include the 'pleasure calculus' or the 'felicific calculus' ('felicific' means to bring about happiness).

> **Hedonic calculus** – devised by Bentham, this involves calculating the amount of pleasure by considering seven key factors about the practical application of pleasure.

Bentham thought there were seven different elements that should be taken into account when calculating the amount of happiness. They are:

1 the intensity of the pleasure – the more intense, the better

2 the duration of the pleasure – the longer lasting, the better

3 the certainty of the pleasure – the more certain that pleasure will result, the better

4 the fecundity (to make fruitful) of the pleasure – the more chance the pleasure will be repeated, or will result in other pleasures, the better

5 the propinquity (nearness) of the pleasure – the nearer the pleasure is to you, the better

6 the purity of the pleasure – the least amount of pain it involves, the better

7 the extent of the pleasure – the more people who experience it, the better.

Using these criteria, Bentham argued that it was possible to work out the right course of action in any situation.

Exam tip

The important thing about Bentham's hedonic calculus is that you understand how it is applied. It is better to remember three elements and explain how they work than to list all seven and not relate them to his theory or an issue.

Now test yourself

4 Explain three aspects of Bentham's hedonic calculus.

5 What other names are given for the calculus?

Answers online

Tested

Mill's Utilitarianism

Quality over quantity

Revised

The ethical theory of Utilitarianism that Bentham proposed soon started to raise some strong criticisms. Not least among the critics was his former pupil, John Stuart Mill. The main criticism against Bentham was that he tried to measure pleasure in quantitative terms. This also raised questions about the exact nature of 'pleasure'.

Mill revised Bentham's form of Utilitarianism by refining it in several ways:

● He revisited the definition of happiness (pleasure) and, similar to Aristotle's idea of '**eudaimonia**', he equated 'happiness' with the idea of what is good, wholesome, fulfilling and virtuous; that which leads to well-being.

● He distinguished between pleasure that stimulated the mind (higher pleasure) and pleasure that was merely physical (lower pleasure). He claimed that human beings alone could achieve the higher pleasures, and it was the higher pleasure that was more satisfying.

● Mill moved the calculation of pleasure away from quantity towards quality. No longer was it just a matter of how much pleasure an action caused. Now it was also a matter of the quality of the pleasure resulting.

● Perhaps the most important contribution by Mill was his introduction of the idea of **universalisability**. Similar to Bentham's principle of utility, Mill wanted to show that what is right and wrong for one person in a situation is right or wrong for all. He argued that:

　○ happiness is desirable (since we all desire it)

　○ happiness is the only thing desirable as an end (things are only desirable because they bring about happiness)

　○ therefore, everyone ought to aim at the happiness of everyone (increasing the general happiness will increase my happiness).

Key quote

'It is better to be a human being dissatisfied than a pig satisfied; better to be Socrates dissatisfied than a fool satisfied.'

(John Stuart Mill)

Eudaimonia – a term used by Aristotle literally meaning 'good spirit' and is translated as 'happiness' or 'well-being'.

Universalisability – something that can apply to everyone.

Typical mistake

Remember not to confuse assessment objectives. AO1 for 30 marks asks you to examine, explain or outline but *not* to assess or evaluate. Do not start to offer personal criticisms of Mill or Bentham if the question asks you to explain their theories.

This argument supports the idea that people should put the interests of the group before their own interests. Bentham's principle of utility had focused on much more individual situations and had no concept of protecting the common good universally.

Now test yourself   Tested ☐

6   State three ways in which Mill's utilitarian theory is different to that of Bentham.

Answer online

> **Exam tip**
>
> In the exam, write a brief bullet list by way of a plan for each question that you attempt to answer. Your bullet list should use key words, for example, for a question on Mill: *refinement of Bentham, higher/lower, quality, eudaimonia, universability.*

Types of Utilitarianism

There are two different forms of Utilitarianism – Act Utilitarianism and Rule Utilitarianism.

Act and Rule Utilitarianism   Revised ☐

Act Utilitarianism

This is usually associated with the Utilitarianism of Bentham and use of his hedonic calculus. Bentham thought that previous experiences did not always help us make moral choices and that each situation was different, and so had to be calculated afresh. Therefore, for **Act Utilitarianism** in its strong form, in each situation the calculus should be applied, regardless of previous experiences in decision making. Since this is the case, Act Utilitarianism appears to favour the individual situations more than the cases for the majority. Although Bentham is said to be an Act Utilitarian, he did not claim that it was necessary to calculate the rightness and wrongness of every act from the hedonic calculus, just that this was generally the case.

> **Act Utilitarianism** – considers the consequence of each individual action.

Rule Utilitarianism

Mill thought previous experiences did help us make decisions. Indeed, human beings have already developed some rules which help them make decisions more quickly. These rules are universal in nature and, if applied in any situation, they would lead to the greatest happiness of the greatest number (i.e. they would maximise happiness). In **Rule Utilitarianism**, moral actions are those which conform to the rules that lead to the greatest good. For example, we do not need to use the hedonic calculus to work out that giving money to the poor is right because it is a well worked rule of Utilitarianism.

> **Rule Utilitarianism** – considers the consequences of past actions to form a rule to guide a present action.

> **Exam tip**
>
> Always be aware of the fact that Bentham and Mill do not neatly fit into the category of Act and Rule Utilitarianism respectively. Good understanding is demonstrated by this awareness.

Mill is said to be a Rule Utilitarian; however, it is doubtful whether he advocated the strong form. He viewed the rules more as helpful guidance than obligatory. They were necessary as a means of saving time. This view, known as weak Rule Utilitarianism, states that on certain occasions the rules can be disobeyed if a greater amount of happiness will result.

Now test yourself

7   Explain the difference between strong and weak Rule Utilitarianism.

8   Why may it be inaccurate to say that Bentham was an Act Utilitarian?

Answers online

Tested ☐

Applying Bentham's and Mill's principles

Approach

In one sense, Utilitarianism is always difficult to apply to any moral issue, because there are never any real absolutes. It is the situation that will affect the decision, and no two situations are identical. However, the key principle in Utilitarianism is 'the greatest happiness of the greatest number'.

When applying Utilitarianism to a moral issue of your choice the most important thing to remember is what Utilitarianism rejects:

- Deontological approach – it is not the action that is intrinsically good or right.
- Act Utilitarianism rejects 'rules'.
- Rule Utilitarianism uses previous experiences to establish patterns of acceptable behaviour that can be applied to situations and rejects the idea that every situation has to be entirely new.

But it is also important to bear in mind that Utilitarianism promotes:

- Bentham's hedonic calculus (see page 9)
- Mill's refinement of 'happiness'
- Mill's idea of higher and lower pleasure
- Mill's understanding of quality over quantity.

Examples

Application of Utilitarianism to a moral issue

Issue	Deontological response, e.g. observation of set moral rules	Utilitarianism: a possible response
War	Do not kill Turn the other cheek	As with most moral issues, the outcomes are difficult to predict with any certainty. This is definitely true of war. The greatest happiness for the greatest number is the criterion used by Utilitarians; however, the calculation of happiness seems an impossible task where a war is involved. One of the key considerations would be the peace that is gained as a result of the war. Put simply, 'does the end justify the means?' The idea of a **just war** may be applicable as it is concerned with just causes and likelihood of success. Bentham's basic ideas of the calculus and Mill's developments could be applied to two main areas: the extent of suffering and the future prospect of peace and prosperity.

Exam tip

In explaining how Utilitarianism may be applied to an issue, try to remember the specific types of principles that are applied as advocated by Bentham and Mill.

Typical mistake

Remember that your selected examples for Utilitarianism cannot be taken from the issues of abortion or euthanasia but must be from a different issue.

Just war – an ancient theory that acknowledges the undesirability of war but yet allows it as a 'lesser of evils' based upon a set of clear principles.

Now test yourself

9 List the five most important key words you would use for applying the Utilitarian theory of Mill to an issue.

Answer online

Exam practice answers at **www.therevisionbutton.co.uk/myrevisionnotes**

Issues arising

Strengths and weaknesses of Bentham and Mill — Revised

Strengths of Utilitarianism that apply to both Bentham and Mill	Weaknesses of Utilitarianism that apply to both Bentham and Mill
It has aims that are attractive – happiness and avoidance of pain. It does seem that we are motivated by pleasure and motivated to avoid pain.	It seems to ignore intentions and an individual's motive. The means by which the greatest good is achieved seems incidental and of no moral relevance. In other words, injustice could be seen as the right action, which seems contrary to common sense.
It seems straightforward to apply to most situations and concurs with common sense.	Because it is concerned with the greater number, the happiness of minorities may not be protected.
It takes into account the consequences of our actions. Looking just at intentions with no regard to their consequence seems impersonal. For instance, keeping someone alive who is terminally ill and suffering great pain ignores the consequences for that person.	In deciding whether an action is morally right, it requires the outcomes of the action to be known. However, outcomes may not be accurately predictable. This is certainly true in the case of a war. It is also true with some forms of genetic engineering.
	To decide what action will produce the greatest good, the alternative actions also have to be considered and their possible outcomes predicted. This seems an impossible task.
It considers others and not just the individual. It is concerned with the common good. It takes into account all who are affected by the action.	Utilitarianism seems too demanding since we ought always to do that which gives greatest good for the greatest number. But there may always be an act, other than what we choose, that would give greater good.

Specific strengths of Bentham	Specific weaknesses of Bentham
It has method in its application of the calculus.	It is not clear how the hedonic calculus resolves the problem of assessing the quantity of pleasure. For instance, how is it possible to quantify and compare intensity of pleasure with duration of pleasure? Listing elements of pleasure does not resolve the problem of quantifying the pleasure.
It is a morally democratic approach that seeks the fairest result.	
The calculus is thorough in its consideration of measuring aspects of pleasure.	The calculus does not prioritise or rank aspects of pleasure and so can lead to confusion.
	Bentham's hedonic calculus appears to justify gang rape.

Specific strengths of Mill	Specific weaknesses of Mill
It is arguably a more intelligent and thoughtful approach than Bentham's theory.	Was Mill right when he argued that higher pleasures are better than lower pleasures?
It avoids the pitfalls of Bentham's basic calculus.	It is too complex a system to calculate.
It comes across as a more refined and nobler system of thought.	Due to its complexity it is therefore of no practical use.

Exam tip

In preparing for a question and answer that involves AO2 assessment and evaluation, try to draw both strengths and weakness with different views. This demonstrates that you have considered more than one point of view.

Now test yourself

10 List two strengths of Utilitarian theory.

11 List two weaknesses of Utilitarian theory.

12 List two strengths of Bentham's Utilitarian theory.

13 List two weaknesses of Mill's Utilitarian theory.

Answers online

Tested

Which is more important – the ending of pain and suffering, or the increase of pleasure?

Revised

This is a key issue for Utilitarianism. First, there is the priority to decide upon. Is it more important to end someone's pain or to satisfy someone's pleasure? In addition, in some moral dilemmas there are no alternatives but those that bring pain and suffering. For example, the lesser of evils situations have no 'happiness' or 'pleasures'. In addition, there are also the usual problems associated with ethical systems that only measure morality according to the consequence of an action. For example 'who makes the decision?' and based upon 'what perspective?', since one person's idea of pleasure and pain may differ from another's.

Arguments in support of and against ending pain and suffering

In support of ending pain and suffering (against the increase of pleasure)	In support of the increase of pleasure (against the ending of pain and suffering)
If pain is great.	Suffering of the few may lead to happiness of the majority, e.g. a just war.
If pain is to be long term and there is no sight of pleasure.	If pain is minimal and the impact of pleasure far supersedes the pain, e.g. allowing torture to save lives.
The quality of pleasure may be poor, e.g. 'lower', and so not worth pursuing.	Depends upon the long-term potential, which may be to allow immediate suffering for greater pleasure later.
If one is already content, why increase contentment at the expense of suffering? This is morally wrong. For example, just because many people are well fed does not mean we should continue to leave the beggar to starve.	

Typical mistake

Remember that this part of the examination process involves assessment or evaluation. To simply repeat what key thinkers say is no good in itself. There also has to be a process of reasoning to your argument and some critical analysis.

How worthwhile is the pursuit of happiness, and is that all that people desire?

Revised

The idea of pursuing happiness as a goal has been called into question. Mill, we have seen, refined this into a nobler idea more akin to Aristotle's eudaimonia. Peter Singer, professor of philosophy, developed this further, influenced by the work of R.M. Hare, another professor of philosophy, and is a major promoter of what is known as **Preference Utilitarianism**. This theory claims that the right thing to do is that which produces the best consequences. However, instead of specifying the end to be pursued in terms of pleasure, it defines the best consequences in terms of preference. This is based on the questions: 'What outcome do I prefer?' 'What is in the best interests of those concerned?' The principle of utility is still followed, so Preference Utilitarianism considers the preferences of all sentient beings. The more preferences satisfied in the world, the better.

Preference Utilitarianism – the idea that the outcome that produces the best result based upon preferences has to be the right course of action to take.

Arguments in support of and against the pursuit of happiness

Supporting the pursuit of happiness	Against the pursuit of happiness
Higher pleasures are noble.	Is happiness or pleasure a valid aim?
Spiritual and intellectual happiness is important.	Depends upon the nature of the happiness.
Happiness is important for complete mental health.	Does it seem rather self-indulgent?
Life is to be enjoyed and not 'suffered'.	What about when pain can be good for you? For example the pain associated with hard work or exercise?
All noble religious and non-religious ideals seek some form of satisfaction.	Preference Utilitarianism.

Exam tip

When revising, write a list of your own questions in response to the issues studied, i.e. lines of argument you would want to pursue.

Typical mistake

Make sure you leave enough time to answer the 15-mark question.

How compatible is Utilitarianism with a religious approach to ethics?

Revised

Compatible	Not compatible
Situation Ethics (see page 16) is similar to Act Utilitarianism, with Mill's refinement of happiness found in the principle of '**agape**'.	Utilitarianism is against the idea of divinely ordained moral codes.
The idea of sacrificing for others is common to many religious traditions.	It is against the ideals of **natural moral law** as adopted by the Roman Catholic tradition.
The Buddhist ideal is to avoid suffering and involves accumulating positive kamma/karma.	The idea of 'means to an end' when it involves people can challenge beliefs about the **sanctity of life**.
The idea of conscience can be related to the calculations of best outcome.	'Means to an end' can be seen to be lacking in compassion.
	What about the religious teachings that concern support of the weak?

Agape – Greek word for love but often translated as 'pure love' or 'unconditional love' to distinguish it from other Greek words for sexual love, friendship and family love.

Natural moral law – the idea that the natural world dictates a moral order discoverable through reason.

Situation Ethics – a theory of ethics according to which moral rules are not absolutely binding but may be modified in the light of specific situations.

Sanctity of life – the belief that life is sacred or holy, given by God.

Exam practice

(a) Explain what is meant by the terms 'Act Utilitarianism' and 'Rule Utilitarianism'. (30 marks)

(b) 'Ending pain and suffering is more important than increasing pleasure.' Assess this view. (15 marks)

Answers online

Online

Exam tip

You don't always have to argue a specific point as a conclusion for AO2. The important thing is to display the skills of evaluation and reasoning. Your conclusion may be that there is no conclusion. You could always end with a question.

1.1 Utilitarianism

1.2 Situation Ethics

The general principles of Situation Ethics

The middle way

American moral theologian, Joseph Fletcher, published a book called *Situation Ethics: The New Morality* in 1966. Fletcher proposed an approach to Christian ethics, called situationism, that considered each situation on its merits before applying the Christian principle of love (**agape**).

It was a middle way that rejected the two extremes of:

- rigidly applying set principles and following laws as absolutes without consideration of context (**legalism**)

- acting without reference to any rules and having total freedom to act as one pleases (**antinomianism**).

It was a theological way of meeting a practical need in light of the radical social changes of the twentieth century; in particular, changing views on what is seen to be acceptable moral behaviour.

> **Agape** – Greek word for love but often translated as 'pure love' or 'unconditional love' to distinguish it from other Greek words for sexual love, friendship and family love.
>
> **Legalism** – set principles are applied as absolutes, regardless of the context.
>
> **Antinomianism** – the freedom of the individual is paramount, regardless of the rules.

The idea of situation

- Fletcher argues that absolute moral principles do not work in the real world.

- An absolute rule or law such as 'it is wrong to kill' is not really treated as an absolute in practice.

- He argues that in order to make a meaningful ethical decision, the situation needs to be considered for each individual moral decision and action.

- In turn, this decision then depends upon the practical application of Christian love (agape).

- The right decision in one circumstance, however, does not become the blueprint for all other circumstances. Each situation should be considered independently.

- Fletcher's approach to ethics was that using absolute ethical principles and applying them to real-life situations was simply not Christian.

> **Typical mistake**
>
> When answering a question on Situation Ethics, try not to be diverted from the question by including too much background detail.

Conscience

Revised

Fletcher's understanding of conscience is different from traditional views; he sees it as a 'function, not as a faculty'. He is not so much interested in what it 'is' as in what it 'does'.

Fletcher rejects what he identifies as the four traditional ideas about conscience: in other words that it is:

1 'an innate, radar-like, built-in faculty – intuition'
2 'inspiration from outside the decision maker – guidance by the Holy Spirit'
3 'the internalised value system of the culture and society' (introjection)
4 'the reason making moral judgements or value choices' (Aquinas).

Fletcher's understanding of the function of conscience is not one of reviewing past actions or apportioning guilt and shame; according to Fletcher, the way conscience functions is by looking forward towards prospective application, that is, the moral problems to solve.

Key quote

'There is no conscience; conscience is merely a word for our attempts to make decisions creatively, constructively, fittingly.'

(Joseph Fletcher)

Making moral decisions rather than following rules

Revised

Fletcher rejects the idea of morality as a manual for the conscience. In other words, morality is not something that is set in stone and dictates how the conscience is to react in a given situation. The Church has made this mistake.

Traditionally, the Church has devised moral principles in abstract, systematised them and then applied them in actual cases to give prescriptions and directives. For example, the principle that to have an abortion is wrong is derived from the ruling found in the Ten Commandments, 'Do not kill'. When a person considers abortion, then, their conscience is dictated to by this directive.

This approach to morality is not life-centred nor person-orientated because it only considers an abstract principle. This is not how Fletcher sees the role of conscience. In contrast, Situation Ethics calls for the practical application of Christian love to a given situation. The situation and context come first and principles are put aside.

Now test yourself

1 Why is situationism described as 'a middle way'?
2 Explain two traditional ideas about conscience that Fletcher rejects.
3 According to Fletcher, why isn't he interested in what conscience 'is'?
4 According to Fletcher, why does 'conscience' seek 'prospective application'?

Answers online

Tested

Fletcher's Situation Ethics

The understanding of Christian love

Revised

The roots of 'new morality' can be found in 'classical' Christianity. Fletcher sees his approach to ethics as grounded in the Christian gospel. He sees love as an active principle – it is a 'doing' thing rather than a noun or thing in itself.

Agape is the word used in the New Testament for pure, unconditional Christian love. It is love which is disinterested and seeks only the benefit of the one who is loved.

Key quote

'Love is the only universal. But love is not something we have or are, it is something we do.'

(Joseph Fletcher)

Four presumptions (working principles)

Fletcher suggested that the effectiveness of Situation Ethics could be tested by his four working principles:

1   **Pragmatism**: The solution to any ethical dilemma has to be practical. Fletcher wrote: 'All are agreed: the good is what works, what is expedient, what gives satisfaction.'

2   **Relativism**: Love (agape love) should be applied in a way that is relative to each individual situation. Fletcher wrote: 'The situationist avoids words such as "never" and "perfect" and "always" and "complete" as he avoids the plague, as he avoids "absolutely".'

3   **Positivism**: Agape is accepted voluntarily through faith, and reason is then used to work out the practical application of that faith. Faith comes first. Moral choices must be vindicated by showing that they work and are based on commitment to agape love.

4   **Personalism**: Ethics concerns itself with people rather than things. The command is to love people and not laws or principles.

> **Pragmatism** – a moral solution is only good if it is practical.
>
> **Relativism** – there is no absolute principle. Every decision depends upon the situation or context.
>
> **Positivism** – statements of faith precede reason.
>
> **Personalism** – ethical theory and morality deal with people first over principles.

Six fundamental principles

Fletcher identifies six statements to serve as basic propositions for the practical application of his ethical theory:

1   Only love is intrinsically good 'Only love is objectively valid, only love is universal.' Fletcher calls it the New Testament's law of love.

2   The ruling norm of Christian decisions is love: nothing else. Laws are mere reflections of love in practice; they are not a set of rules but a guide derived from previous applications of love: 'the Sabbath was made for man and not man for the Sabbath'. The situationist recognises the law for what it is and no more.

3   Love and justice are the same, for justice is love distributed, nothing else. If justice is to give human beings what they deserve, then one cannot say that one truly loves if the outcome is not just.

4   Love wills the neighbour's good whether we like him or not. Jesus urged everyone to 'love your enemies', meaning, for Fletcher, the radical obligation of showing 'indiscriminate love, love for Tom, Dick and Harry'. Pure love does not discriminate in its application.

5   Only the end justifies the means, nothing else. Fletcher argues that Situation Ethics deals with end results. To follow absolutes is impossible. For example, to follow the principle 'do not kill' for an absolutist is not practical and at some point the 'inflexible maxims' (absolutes) are compromised or made flexible, e.g. war, abortion, self-defence, animal rights.

6   Love's decisions are made situationally, not prescriptively. For real decision making, freedom is required. Fletcher's clear conclusion is that all ethical decisions must be situation-based (led, of course, by agape) and not principle-based.

> **Exam tip**
>
> Make sure that when you answer a question on Situation Ethics you explain each key term you use. You can do this by selecting appropriate examples and evidence. You must do this to reach Level 6.

> **Typical mistake**
>
> It is vital to learn the key terms for a topic. To demonstrate the highest levels of understanding, it is important not to confuse the terms. Remember, it is far better to use a few correctly rather than many inaccurately.

> **Now test yourself**
>
> 5   Match each of the following phrases with one of Fletcher's four presumptions:
>   *Situation Ethics is about faith*
>   *Situation Ethics is always considerate of the circumstances*
>   *Situation Ethics has people as its main concern*
>   *Situation Ethics is always practical*
>
> 6   Explain what the following terms mean for Fletcher: (a) agape, (b) justice.
>
> Answers online

Application to an ethical issue

Approach ——————————————————————— Revised □

When applying Situation Ethics to a moral issue of your choice, the most important thing to remember is the approach of Situation Ethics and what it rejects:

- legalism
- antinomianism.

But you also need to bear in mind what it promotes:

- a focus on a practical application of Christian love (agape)
- a clear consideration of the situation and use of conscience as a forward-looking means of assessment
- an assessment of the outcome, as the end justifies the means
- a focus on the person involved as a priority, ahead of any absolutes that may impinge upon this
- that the end is just and reflects the neighbour's good.

For example:

Issue	Absolutes to avoid	Situation Ethics: a possible response
Pacifism	Do not kill Turn the other cheek	Once again, agape is strong when required and if the ends are neither just nor will the good of neighbours, then it cannot be the correct action. Therefore, if war is in self-defence and for the benefit of human beings in the long term, action must be taken – as 'turning the other cheek' or following the principle 'do not kill' without considering the outcome would be a grave injustice.

Many other examples could be given but the above indicates how Situation Ethics works in practice.

In addition, it must be remembered that each case and situation is an individual one and should never form a blueprint for another decision. In the example of using violence, in particular, there are many complicated situations that could merit either a move for violence or a call for pacifism.

Issues arising

When Fletcher's book first appeared it was met with much opposition from many different people and groups within Christianity. It was not, however, until a few years later that there was an official written critique by the biblical scholar and theologian William Barclay in his book *Ethics for a Permissive Society*. Both the strengths and weaknesses of Situation Ethics need to be considered.

> **Exam tip**
>
> In explaining how Situation Ethics may be applied to an issue, use the working principles and the six propositions to help consider how the application of agape works.

> **Typical mistake**
>
> Remember that your selected examples for Situation Ethics cannot be taken from the issues of abortion or euthanasia but must be from another different issue.

> **Now test yourself**
>
> 7 Identify two key religious or moral absolutes for each of the following issues: (a) a Christian being asked to go to war, (b) having a child through IVF to save a sibling because of genetic illness.
>
> 8 List three things to consider when applying the theory of Situation Ethics.
>
> Answers online
>
> Tested □

Strengths and weaknesses of Situation Ethics as an ethical system

Revised ☐

Strengths	Weaknesses
It fits in with the whole 'philosophy' and practical ethics of Jesus in the New Testament. Jesus broke religious rules and dealt with everyone as individuals and according to the circumstances.	There will always be a dispute as to what really is the most loving thing to do, and what this actually means in practice.
	Fletcher's views do not necessarily accurately reflect New Testament views on morality (e.g. the New Testament appears to have clear moral views on theft and adultery).
It is flexible in that it gives personal freedom to people to decide what is the most loving action.	The examples Fletcher uses to justify Situation Ethics are so extreme that they account for very few real instances in life.
Situation Ethics does not reject laws but sees them as useful tools which are not absolutely binding.	William Barclay argued that if law is 'the distillation of experience' that society has found to be beneficial, then 'to discard law is to discard experience' and the valuable wisdom and insight it may bring.
The 'situationism' of Fletcher has been instrumental in, for example, the Church of England (among others) recognising areas of possible injustice, such as the issues of equality, the role of women in the Church and slavery.	The law and absolutes are there for the protection of society. This is the reason they exist.
There can only be a Christian basis of morality if agape love is seen as central to morality. In other words, if we follow how love guides us then how can it be wrong?	Situation Ethics seems to deconstruct itself. We need a specific or definitive idea of what outcome is most valued, best or right before we can decide upon which acts are needed to bring about that right.

Exam tip

In preparing for a question and answer that involves AO2 assessment and evaluation, try to draw both strengths and weaknesses from a variety of sources. This demonstrates that you have considered more than one point of view.

Typical mistake

To simply repeat what Barclay, for example, says is no good in itself. There also has to be a process of reasoning to your argument and some critical analysis.

If love is the highest Christian law and overrules all others when necessary, does this mean that love allows people to do anything?

Revised ☐

While much of Fletcher's Situation Ethics was pitted against legalism, there is another side of the coin – getting rid of absolutes could actually promote liberalism, antinomianism or a freedom to justify any action under the guise of love. William Barclay observed this.

This is the basis of the next evaluation of whether the freedom Situation Ethics promotes is too excessive.

Evaluating Situation Ethics and the extent of freedom

Yes, it does allow people to do anything	No, it does not allow people to do anything
To abandon rules is dangerous: 'freedom can become licence; freedom can become selfishness and even cruelty' and therefore anything can be justified (Barclay).	Agape is, for all intents and purposes, the quality control aspect of Situation Ethics. It is faith in agape that does not allow anything but the most loving outcome.
Barclay was uncomfortable with Fletcher's view that nothing is intrinsically good or bad in itself. Barclay always attested that a bad action could never in any circumstance become a good one.	It is strongly argued by Fletcher that it is the concept of agape as the 'ruling norm' of Christianity that therefore means that the only actions that can be justified are ones driven through love.
When Fletcher defines situations, such situations themselves are interpreted by whoever sees them. Then whoever sees them interprets them according to their own values and theories. This weakens agape and means that any action, given the possibility of any present and future context, could be ethically justified.	Laws are the distillation of experience and have been formulated through agape. It is only when we distil them and use them as blueprints that they become devoid of love. Reformulation and application of agape always supersedes previous cases.
Fletcher is not totally consistent in his description of love. One critic charged that the term 'love' runs through the book like a 'greased pig', while others accused him of 'sloppy agape' (Childress).	To say that 'anything can be justified' is meaningless and demonstrates a total lack of understanding of the fundamental distinction between an antinomian and a situationist.

Exam practice answers at **www.therevisionbutton.co.uk/myrevisionnotes**

How practical is Situation Ethics?

- Situation Ethics is too complex to be of any practical use and therefore is only for those who are able fully to understand, apply and use it accurately, appropriately and effectively.
- It is not practical for society due to a confusion that emerges between what is good and what is right.
- Barclay recognises the value of flexibility in a situationist approach; however, 'we do well still to remember that there are laws which we break at our peril'.

- Fletcher never demanded that an ethical decision should become law; the whole point of Situation Ethics is against this idea. Therefore, issues of right and wrong always remain relative. Just because something is seen to be appropriate in one case does not mean it is justified in all cases, or that it is right *per se*; love deems it to be fitting and appropriate for the circumstance, it meets the needs of the moment. In this sense Situation Ethics is much more practical than any other ethical approach because it is realistic.

Exam tip

When evaluating, try to raise your own questions in response to the issues studied.

Is Situation Ethics compatible with other Christian approaches to moral decision making?

Fletcher claimed that his approach to ethics was grounded in Christianity. How far, then, does Situation Ethics relate to other Christian approaches to ethics?

It is compatible	It is incompatible
Agape makes it compatible with any Christian approach that sees 'love' as the centre of Christianity. Jesus himself broke the Sabbath law on work in favour of a person-centred approach when he plucked 'heads of grain to eat' on the Sabbath when he and his disciples were hungry.	In 1956, the study of the situationist approach to ethics (referred to as 'new morality') was banned from all Roman Catholic academies and seminaries on the grounds of its incompatibility with Roman Catholic teaching. Barclay's official critique also supported incompatibility.
The change in views within Christianity on issues such as war, slavery, the death penalty and equality for women indicates recognition that absolutes are not always absolute.	There are clear fundamental laws and absolutes in the Bible that many Christians adhere to when making moral decisions.
Christians may follow theories such as **Utilitarianism** that have some similarities with Situation Ethics.	Kant's categorical imperative, which is based in rules that are 'set', and the underpinning principles of Natural Law that point out we can work out a definitive course of action through reason, are certainly not compatible with Situation Ethics.

Now test yourself

9 List three weaknesses of Situation Ethics.

10 List three strengths of Situation Ethics.

11 Give one reason why Situation Ethics is practical.

12 Give one reason why Situation Ethics is not practical.

Answers online

Tested

Utilitarianism – argues that the correct way of action is derived from working out what brings happiness to the greatest number. See page 8.

Exam practice

(a) Outline Fletcher's main teachings on Situation Ethics. **(30 marks)**

(b) 'Situation Ethics cannot be considered a Christian approach to ethics.' Assess this view. **(15 marks)**

Answers online

Online

1.3 Religious teaching on the nature and value of human life

Nature of humanity and the human condition

When it comes to exploring the question 'What does it mean to be human?', there are three main aspects to any answer:

- the *nature* of being human, meaning the traditional definition of body and soul/mind
- the *status* of being human, meaning the significance of humanity in relation to others
- the *purpose* of being human, meaning the expectations that being human involves.

For each of these three aspects, there is no single unified answer. All answers to such 'ultimate questions' are related to particular world views or perspectives, both religious and non-religious.

What it means to be human: the nature of being human

Revised

Non-religious views

A non-religious answer would point out that since there is no creator, i.e. God, human beings are not 'created beings'. Life has evolved over millions of years. The idea of a 'spiritual' aspect to humanity is rejected, and non-religious views speak of a 'mind' and not a soul. Richard Dawkins writes, 'There is no spirit-driven life force, no throbbing, heaving, pullulating, protoplasmic, mystic jelly. Life is just bytes and bytes and bytes of digital information' (*River out of Eden*, 1995). Such a view is often referred to as materialism, recognising the holistic nature of mind and body.

In a recent scientific book entitled *What is Your Dangerous Idea?*, the psychologist John Hogan discusses the 'search for the **neural code**' and points out that materialist thinkers are trying to demonstrate beyond all doubt that the idea of the soul is dead. There is research in modern psychology to pinpoint the physical origins of **neurosis**, almost like a DNA of the mind that originates with our physical properties. If such a code were discovered, then all need for a mystical soul would be eradicated.

> **Neural code** – the physical explanation for mental formations.
>
> **Neurosis** – any sort of physical behaviour or symptom that has no physical cause but a cause that is rooted in the mind.

Christianity

The nature of humanity in Christian teaching goes back to the book of Genesis in the Old Testament and the story of how the Christian God created the world. Within this, human beings were created from the earth – 'from the of dust of the ground' (Genesis 2:7) – and in this respect are physical entities; however, their existence also bears the mark of the creator:

God 'breathed into his nostrils the breath of life, and the man became a living being' (Genesis 2:7). In other words, while physical entities, human beings also have a spiritual aspect that is God-given. This is the 'soul' or 'spirit' and, while most Christians accept the existence of a soul, there has been much debate within Christianity as to what this actually is. The main understanding appears to be that it is both 'spiritual in essence' and 'immortal'.

Some scholars claim that in the New Testament there is little indication that human beings are naturally immortal. Only God is described in such terms. In other words, the emphasis is on the unity of a person. Actions we take in this life involve both body and soul. It is an act of the whole person. Some thinkers have taken this even further. For example, the theologian John Hick takes a materialist stance and rejects the immortality of the soul because he sees the mind or soul as integral to what a human being is. However, he does not reject immortality outright, just as the materialist Buddhist does not reject the afterlife; Hick proposes another world after death involving **resurrection** as a whole and explains this through his 'replica' theory.

> **Resurrection** – to come back from the dead.

Despite this, there does seem to be clear reference in the Bible to an immaterial part of a person – a soul and/or spirit, as well as the physical body.

Paul refers to the spirit as something independent of our thought processes. 'For if I pray in a tongue, my spirit prays, but my mind is unfruitful' (1 Corinthians 14:14). He also indicates that he believed that, after death, his spirit would go into the Lord's presence: 'We are confident, I say, and would prefer to be away from the body and at home with the Lord' (2 Corinthians 5:8). Revelation 20:4 refers to souls: 'And I saw the souls of those who had been beheaded because of their testimony for Jesus and because of the word of God.'

What it means to be human: the status of being human

Revised

Non-religious views

Status, according to a scientific view, is that position we have derived for ourselves as a species within the process of evolution. We are *homo sapien* and part of the great ape family. We have evolved our own niche within the tapestry of life. As a species, we consider ourselves top of the order of beings. Any hint of divine activity within this process is rejected as we are simply carriers of DNA. It is our genetic make-up, or DNA, that becomes the 'soul' of our lives. Our sense of self and individuality has its basis in digital information, in genes working together to give a sense of being human.

Christianity

Human beings were created in the 'image' and after the 'likeness' of God (Genesis 1:26). They therefore have a very special status. Although lower than angels and higher than animals, it is the fact that they have a soul that brings uniqueness. In the creation stories of Genesis it can be clearly seen that human beings are the pinnacle of God's creation and were given **'dominion'** on the planet.

> **Dominion** – in Christianity, a word meaning responsibility for the created world.

Originally, human beings were created without sin, but with free will. Adam and Eve disobeyed God, and through sin brought death and imperfection into the world. The relationship between humanity and God was broken. Some refer to this as the 'fall' and it has been traditional Christian teaching that we were all present seminally in the sin of Adam and so we all inherit a sinful nature.

Despite this, part of the status of humanity, being the most cherished of God's creation, is that humans have the opportunity to be redeemed through accepting the grace and forgiveness of God that is available through Jesus Christ (Son of God), who has atoned for their mistakes through becoming 'flesh' (incarnation) and suffering and dying for their sins only be resurrected and re-establish the order of creation.

What it means to be human: the purpose of being human

Revised

Non-religious views

Scientists such as Dawkins tend to reject the idea of **teleological purpose**, that is, the idea that the human race and life itself has a goal towards which it is working and which is driven from the beginning. Life is about survival and populating. Life involves a fight in which the fittest survive. This is the purpose for humanity if there is one and it is purely biological in explanation, not metaphysical. Life on Earth has no future purpose other than helping to determine the global evolving of the planet. Human beings are to express purpose in life by contributing to the whole.

Christianity

In essence, the purpose of a human being is to worship and enjoy God. The idea of a 'relationship' between God and humanity is seen in the Judeo-Christian tradition through ideas of covenant and chosen people, later fulfilled through the sacrifice of Jesus. In its infancy the relationship involves a betrayal and disobedience on the part of humanity; however, the purpose of humanity is to achieve its potential as sons and daughters of God through the new covenant established through Jesus Christ. It is a **redemption** through forgiveness and the **atonement** for sins by Jesus' selfless act of suffering and dying for humanity. The practical outcome of this re-established relationship is that human beings are to fulfil the original criteria of worshipping and enjoying God, following God's teachings as directed in the holy books and maintaining the belief in Jesus as the Son of God. The final purpose is eternal salvation.

Fatalism and free will

There has always been the debate within philosophy, ethics and religion as to the extent of personal responsibility and the ability to choose our own path (free will) in life, as opposed to the influence and intervention of factors beyond our control – whether these be divine agents or universal forces or principles.

> **Teleological** – an ethical theory that considers the consequences of a particular action, or the 'end' result, and it is the assessment of this 'end' that determines whether or not the action is morally good.
>
> **Redemption** – to be brought back. In Christian terms, to be delivered from sin.
>
> **Atonement** – making up for wrongdoing; the reconciliation of man with God through the life, suffering and the sacrificial death of Christ.

Typical mistake

Candidates often get technical religious words mixed up. To avoid this, prepare thoroughly and create your own religious language cards.

Now test yourself

1 What are the three aspects relevant to the human condition?

2 What is Jesus' selfless act of suffering and dying known as?

3 According to a non-religious view, what is the purpose of life?

4 What is the Christian understanding of the relationship between humanity and God?

5 What does the term 'fall' mean in Christian understanding?

Answers online

Tested

Human beings and destiny

The role of God: predestination and determinism

- For **non-religious people** it is thought that free will is inherent to the human condition. For people such as Richard Dawkins, an individual makes choices that are free from any divine influence at all. However, within philosophy there remains the debate about whether or not our actions are determined by outside factors and influences.

- Within religion there is the same debate. For example, how do we know that we have free will and are free to choose when God is almighty, has ultimate power and control and knows everything? This apparent logical contradiction has been debated within religion for centuries. In Christianity the principles are the same. It developed different schools of thought regarding the extent of a human being's freedom.

  - **Christians** have often disagreed about the role of human free will. Armenians taught that all human beings have total free will. Luther believed that sin had so clouded the human mind that our free will was severely restricted and that only by grace could we turn to God. Based upon the teachings of Ephesians 1:4 – 'For he chose us in him before the creation of the world to be holy and blameless in his sight' – John Calvin proposed that we are totally predestined.

Human endeavours and potential

- **Non-religious**: Despite not acknowledging a divine controller or a teleological end to life, those that are non-religious still have a view that human life has much value and potential. Richard Dawkins still believes in human dignity and individual purpose. The problem with religion is that it seeks for an answer to life beyond life. For Dawkins, this is irrational; it is more appropriate to think as a scientist and reason based upon evidence. The fact that human beings have evolved to the point of actually searching for meaning in life is wonderful in itself, creation myth apart. It is not relevant to worry about the meaning of the whole and our place in a hostile universe because we 'are' the universe. As human beings we have the greatest status and intellect on the planet and have the power to shape our own destiny as a species. Our genes manipulate on the biological level but it is our **memes** (memories of key ideas), such as from the sciences and arts, that develop us collectively as a species. Morality is not revealed to human beings by some divine being but worked out biologically through the whole process of evolution and a utilitarian-like appeal to that which suits the majority.

> **Exam tip**
>
> When answering a question on the human condition, try to demonstrate that you understand that there are specific aspects and specific views about this topic. You can do this by using examples to support your answer.

> **Key quote**
>
> 'We ourselves are responsible for our own deeds, happiness and misery. We build our own hells. We create our own heavens. We are the architects of our own fate. In short we ourselves are our own Karma.'
>
> (Narada Thera, Buddhist monk)

> **Memes** – memories or ideas that are inherited; a term invented by Dawkins to refer to a unit of cultural inheritance.

1.3 Religious teaching on the nature and value of human life

- **Christianity**: The endeavours of the human condition for Christians are to fulfil their true nature; that is, to develop in our 'likeness' of God (Genesis 1:26). Until the time of Jesus (who brought a message of forgiveness and reconciliation to God), humans were given the Ten Commandments to try and follow, living as God would want them to. The teachings of Jesus are also of great significance to the Christian journey through life. Jesus came to complete or fulfil the religious law of Judaism (Matthew 5:17). His teachings on law and behaviour can be summarised by two statements:

  ○ 'Love the Lord your God with all your heart and with all your soul and with all your strength and with all your mind; and, your neighbour as yourself' (Luke 10:27). This is known as the **'Greatest Commandment'** and it can be found in the story of the Good Samaritan.

  ○ 'So in everything, do to others what you would have them do to you, for this sums up the Law and the Prophets.' (Matthew 7:12). This is known as the **'Golden Rule'** and can be found in the Sermon on the Mount.

Some of most influential teachings of Jesus are from the Sermon on the Mount, found in the Gospel of Matthew, which is actually several teachings grouped together. They are considered to be the essence of Jesus' teaching on morality. Throughout the 'sermon' Jesus highlights the need for careful thought and reflection before an action and he also points out the hypocrisy of judging others who have done wrong when our own thoughts and failings prove that no one is perfect except God. Martin Luther said the Sermon on the Mount was there to show us how weak we are as human beings; other people have said that it was not a rule book for Christians or for society, but is simply a guide for individual believers as they aim to fulfil their potential as Christians.

Exam tip

Remember to explain each point that you make in an exam answer to the full. Think carefully about each sentence and how it relates to the question and the previous sentence. Aim for at least three sentences to explain a point. For example, state what the teaching is, how it is understood and then give an example.

Now test yourself

Tested ☐

6 State two different schools that hold views about predestination.

7 Explain, with examples, two ways in which Christians can fulfil their potential as human beings.

8 From a non-religious view, how important is free will?

Answers online

Key quotes

'Blessed are the peacemakers, for they shall be called sons of God.'

(Matthew 5:9)

'Let your light shine before men, that they may see your good deeds and praise your father in heaven.'

(Matthew 5:16)

'You have heard that it was said to the people long ago "Do not murder"... But I tell you that anyone where is angry with his brother will subject to judgement.'

(Matthew 5:21, 22)

'You have heard that it was said, "Do not commit adultery." But I tell you that anyone who looks at a women lustfully has already committed adultery with her in his heart.'

(Matthew 5:27, 28)

'You have heard that it was said, "An eye for an eye."... if someone strikes you on the right check, turn to him the other also.'

(Matthew 5:38, 39)

'You have heard also that it was said, "Love your neighbour and hate your enemy." But I tell you: love your enemy and pray for those who persecute you, that you may be sons of your father in heaven. He causes his sun to rise on the evil and the good.'

(Matthew 5:43–45)

'Do not judge or you too will be judged.'

(Matthew 7:1)

Greatest Commandment – to love God and love one's neighbour.

Golden Rule – a phrase used for Jesus' teachings on how we treat others.

Typical mistake

Make sure that you focus on the question carefully when planning and writing your answer and avoid including irrelevant material.

Equality and difference

It is often the case within religion that equality is fought for because it is just. However, there is also a recognition that people are different. Nonetheless, it is widely recognised that such differences do not impact upon the basic tenet that all are equal before God.

Religious teaching about race
Revised

Christianity

Many see Jesus as someone who promoted racial harmony. He often showed himself to be against discrimination. He associated with groups usually considered outcasts. As well as this, Jesus ignored Jewish ideas on pollution by sharing a cup with a Samaritan. The New Testament teaches that within the Christian Church there is neither Greek nor Jew, but 'all one in Christ Jesus' (Galatians 3:26–28).

The human race is seen as one.

Other examples of Christian teaching that promote racial harmony include the Golden Rule: 'Treat others as you would wish to be treated'. The parable of the Good Samaritan teaches to treat everyone with kindness and compassion. Christians also follow Jesus' example by trying not to judge others. On top of all this, there is also the general idea of **agape** – compassion and self-sacrificial love. All these Christian teachings promote racial harmony.

> **Agape** – Greek word for love but often translated as 'pure love' or 'unconditional love' to distinguish it from other Greek words for sexual love, friendship and family love.

Religious teaching about gender
Revised

Christianity

There are many different attitudes within Christianity to the roles of men and women. For example, the Roman Catholic Church and the Orthodox Church have a traditional view on the role of women. Women are not allowed to become priests within these traditions. One reason is because Jesus' apostles were all men. Protestant Churches have within them a mixture of conservative and liberal views about the role of women in Christian ordained ministry.

In the New Testament, Paul wrote: 'The man is the head of the woman, as Christ is the head of the church'. Therefore, those who follow this view will have a more traditional view of the role of women. Women were nonetheless regarded as important to both Jesus and Paul. Both had good friendships with women and women were the earliest witnesses of the resurrection.

Ultimately, the attitudes to the role of men and women are dependent upon which Christian tradition is followed.

Religious teaching about disability
Revised

Given that in Christianity the general human condition is one of a sinful disposition then the very basic view of humanity involves disability on a spiritual level. Historically, within religions, there has been the unfortunate ignorant association of outward physical conditions with inner spiritual health. In addition, mental disabilities were often seen to be 'demonic'! Such thinking is unfounded both morally and theologically.

The basic stance of all faiths is that while humanity has great potential, the starting point should be one of humility and recognition of an imperfect condition. Once this is established it is clear to see that there is a tradition of compassion and duty of care towards the weak or oppressed that permeates Christianity. In all situations, the strong should support the weak with compassion. This would include all people in the following categories: those with disabilities, both physical and mental; those who are terminally ill; those in poverty; those who are oppressed.

Key teachings include:

- the Golden Rule: 'Treat others as you would wish to be treated'
- the Greatest Commandment: 'Love God with all your heart, soul, mind and strength and love your neighbour as you love yourself'
- agape: the Christian application of unconditional love that is indiscriminate.

> **Exam tip**
>
> This section is full of new concepts. In your revision, instead of just drawing up a glossary of key words, try changing this into a flowchart that links each aspect of the topic together.

> **Typical mistake**
>
> Do not get the issues mixed up. If you are asked about race, do not digress into gender: remain focused. If you are asked about race, do not digress into gender: remain focused.

> **Now test yourself**
>
> 9 Give two views about attitudes to race.
>
> 10 Give two views about attitudes to gender.
>
> 11 Give two views about attitudes to disability.
>
> Answers online
>
> Tested

The value of life

In all situations, human life has the quality assurance of God. This would include all people in the following categories: those with disabilities; those who are terminally ill; those in poverty; those who are oppressed. It is the duty of a human being to act positively towards human life.

Religious teaching about the value and quality of life
Revised

Christianity

Christians believe that God is the creator and has almighty power. Man is seen as being created in God's image to rule over everything in creation. This means that Christians see their role in preserving the creation as very important. They believe that all humankind has the responsibility to act as the servants of God and to practise the idea of **stewardship**. Stewardship is the Christian belief that you should act with responsibility: man cannot do as he likes – he must respect life, as all life has been created by God and is therefore sacred and precious. The Ten Commandments show that man has a duty to God and to others; for example, 'Do not kill' shows that life has a value and no man has the right to take it. It also shows that no life is disposable and everyone has a value and a purpose. As all mankind is the family of God then all are equal so no one's life has more value than that of another. It also means that all have the duty to care for one another – which ties in with stewardship, as all are part of the creation.

> **Stewardship** – a duty to look after and care for something on behalf of somebody else.

Religious teaching about self-sacrifice

Revised

Teachings of self-sacrifice are prevalent within Christianity. The very basis of Christian teaching is the sacrifice made by Jesus. Christians are encouraged to follow in the footsteps of Jesus. The key teachings above also underline the importance of self-sacrifice. The whole rationale behind the idea of self-sacrifice is that there is a greater good and that physical existence is only the partial picture.

> **Exam tip**
>
> Be careful when using quotes. Make sure that the quote relates to the material that is presented. To make sure of this, always explain the relevance of the quote in your answer.

Religious teaching about the value and quality of non-human life

Revised

Christianity

The Genesis story clearly states that God created the world and it was 'good'. Despite this, human beings are still the most important of creation. However, this does not mean that the rest of creation is worthless. On the contrary, other creatures are witness to the glory of God, although the traditional Christian teaching is that they do not have souls nor the capacity to reason. Some modern Christian thinking gives a greater value to animals, pointing out that God made a covenant with them as well and that the Garden of Eden, as a picture of the ideal world, gives them peace and security as much as humanity.

> **Now test yourself**
>
> 12 How does creation highlight the importance of non-human life in Christianity?
>
> 13 Give one example of why animal life is valuable for a Christian.
>
> 14 Give one teaching from Christianity of self-sacrifice.
>
> **Answers online**
>
> Tested

Issues arising

How far must a religious view of life be fatalistic?

Revised

This issue is the traditional debate within religions between the idea of free will, human accountability and human responsibility, in contrast to the idea of predestination, fatalism or determinism.

Arguments in support of and against the recognition of free will

In support	Against
The teaching of predestination supports a fatalistic view of life.	Any form of free will suggests a lack of divine planning.
Some religious traditions support this, e.g. Calvinist (Christian).	Free will challenges traditional ideas about God.
Some find a semi-fatalistic view, e.g. Arminian (Christian).	If human beings are judged by God then there must be free will or judgement makes no sense.

> **Exam tip**
>
> Always make sure that you draw a conclusion from the arguments that you have put forward. This does not necessarily have to agree with an argument. Your conclusion may be that questions are unanswered.

How far can religion support the idea of equality?

There is no doubt that in theory all religions can support the idea of equality. Spiritually everyone is given equal status before God and the sanctity-of-life teaching promotes this equality. However, in reality, there are clear suggestions of inequality.

Exam tip

When revising, use different coloured pens to compare and contrast different lines of argument.

Arguments in support of and against the idea of equality in religion

In support	Against
God created all – sanctity of life (Christian).	There have been issues of gender inequality. For example, Paul's view of the role of women.
The Holy Spirit is within all and so we all contain divine essence.	The Roman Catholic Church does not allow women to be priests.
God cares for all creation.	Religion may sometimes be used to promote racial inequality.
Female religious leaders exist today.	There are clear roles and some have more authority, e.g. leaders.

Can religion accept priority of human life over non-human life?

This is a crucial issue for religions today. Philosophers such as Peter Singer argue that all life is of value and humans have no more rights than animals.

Arguments in support of and against the priority of human life

In support	Against
Christianity teaches that humans have been given dominion.	Stewardship does not necessarily imply superiority in terms of value.
Christianity teaches that humans have souls and animals do not.	Dominion or stewardship does not necessarily mean 'priority'.
Christianity teaches that humans are stewards and have special status.	Vegetarians may argue that we are morally inferior if we eat other creatures.
Humans are spiritually more advanced than animals.	It is stated in the Bible that God cares for all creation.
The human condition is unique and has the potential for salvation.	
Issues such as animal testing and experimentation imply superiority.	

Exam tip

Your answer should always select the key points and arguments – that is, the appropriate information relevant to the question. This demonstrates more personal understanding or 'ownership' of the issue and will help you to draw clear conclusions.

Can religion accept priority of some human life as more valuable than others?

Revised ☐

Are all human beings equal? This issue focusses on the debate involving inequality in terms of gender but also regarding disability.

Arguments in support of and against the prioritisation of some human life over others

In support	Against
The whole idea of judgement demonstrates that some will be rejected by God, e.g. the parable of the sheep and the goats.	All are equal before God.
A holy person is seen as much more spiritually developed than anyone else.	All have within them an aspect of the divine.
The debate about the role of women can be seen to suggest that Christianity promotes men over women.	To claim superiority or priority would be against religious teachings.

Exam tip

Always refer back to the question in your answers, demonstrating that you comprehend the demand of the question for AO2.

Exam practice

(a) Explain what religion means when it talks about 'the value of life'.

(30 marks)

(b) 'People are different and so cannot be treated the same.' Assess this view.

(15 marks)

Answers online

Online ☐

1.4 Abortion and euthanasia

Abortion

The issue of abortion is complex. Debate can be emotive, with strong feelings of justice and injustice often aroused.

An abortion can be defined as the termination of a pregnancy before 24 weeks. Abortions are available on the NHS but women seeking them must be referred by a doctor.

The guidelines are outlined in the 1967 Abortion Act (see page 36).

The start of human life — Revised

The initial problem for the abortion debate is in establishing the point at which human life begins. This is not universally agreed and there are different explanations for this, whether biological, philosophical or religious. The point at which human life begins has a direct impact upon the views about abortion in several ways:

- If a **fetus** is not a human being then it may not have the same rights as a fully independent human being and need not have the same kind of protection in law.
- If human life begins at conception then, in theory, a fetus should have the same rights afforded to a fully independent human being in law.
- If this is the case, is the point at which human rights for it may begin the point at which a fetus becomes human during pregnancy.
- If the point at which a fetus becomes human is during pregnancy, then this could lead to a conflict of rights between the mother and the unborn child.

> **Fetus** – the unborn baby from the end of the eighth week after conception (when the major structures have formed) until birth.

Key quote

'Personhood may be one thing and human life another; hence it is possible to argue that, while the zygote may not be a person, there is no logical alternative to regarding it as the first stage in human life.'

(Mason and Laurie, professors of law)

Biological debates — Revised

Biological debates depend upon physical evidence to define the status of the fetus.

'When does human life begin?'

This biological data can be interpreted in different ways in relation to the question 'When does human life begin?' The following stages are often put forward as key points for the beginning of human life:

- **Birth:** the status of **personhood** is only applied at actual physical birth, the first true point of independence and individuality.
- **Viability:** the status of personhood is awarded at that time when the unborn can exist beyond any dependence on the mother.

> **Personhood** – the stage at which a being is considered to be an individual human being with human rights.

- **Potentiality:** this has different meanings but basically implies the point at which the entity displays the potential of becoming a human being – for some this may be at the moment of conception, for others the primitive streak and for others the quickening.
  - The primitive streak is discernible after the fourteenth day in the development of the fetus and it is this that becomes the spinal cord.
  - Quickening: this is a traditional understanding that the status of personhood can be applied when the 'child' is first felt to move.
- **Conception:** from the point of fertilisation of the egg (conception) the resulting product is a human being.

Philosophical and religious debates

Revised

Philosophical or religious arguments are based on concepts or principles beyond the physical evidence, that is, the **metaphysical** issues.

- **Consciousness:** the status of personhood is applied at the first point of consciousness or awareness.
- **Ensoulment:** the status of personhood is deemed appropriate when the soul enters the body.
- **Continuity:** life must begin when the potential life as an individual entity is recognisable, which is the zygote at conception.
- **Relational factors:** all arguments are based upon the meaning of words, or what the philosopher Peter Vardy calls 'relational factors'. That is, there are different interpretations or understandings of the same words. Until accurate definitions of key terms are agreed, the stage at which personhood status is awarded can never be universal.

Different stages for different humans?

Finally, there is a clear disparity in the development of individuals. During life, although there are broad timescales at which people mature, develop and grow, there is, by the very nature of individuality, a blurring of the exact moment one moves from adolescence to adulthood, from childhood through puberty and so forth. Why are the early stages of development any different?

> **Metaphysical** – relating to a reality beyond what is perceptible to the senses.

> **Exam tip**
> Any answers to the question 'When does human life start?' should show awareness of the condition of the unborn in each definition chosen and explain why this stage in development has been identified as the start of life.

The value of potential life: different views

Revised

The key debates on abortion consider at which point potential human life acquires such value as to make abortion an ethical injustice. As Peter Singer, the philosopher, writes, 'To kill a human adult is murder, and is unhesitatingly and universally condemned. Yet there is no obvious sharp line which marks the zygote from the adult. Hence the problem.' This then leads into more specific questions concerning the nature and status of the fetus.

There are different ways of understanding the 'value of potential life':

- The **sanctity of life**, which is the belief that life is in some way sacred or holy, traditionally understood as being given by God.
- The philosopher Kant gives the idea of the sanctity of life a non-religious perspective based on purely ethical grounds.

> **Key quote**
> 'The basic argument against abortion, on which all others build, is that the unborn child is already a human being, a person, a bearer of rights, and that abortion is therefore murder.'
> (John Leslie Mackie)

> **Sanctity of life** – the belief that life is sacred or holy, given by God.

Since consciousness and reason are not properties of potential life, then its value diminishes accordingly. In other words, personhood is based upon the ability to reason.

● Philosophers such as Peter Singer have long called for a shift from talking about the sanctity of life towards a more universal discussion about the value of life. Singer does not create a ringfence around humanity, but instead talks about the value of all living things.

● Some scientists would argue that, although the fetus does not have person status or human rights and is purely a part of the process of survival of the fittest, this does not mean it has no value. It is the process of evolution and the fetus' place within it – whether it survives or not – that gives the fetus its value.

● Tony Hope, professor of medical ethics, in his book *Medical Ethics and Law*, raises an important point about the interests of a potential child when dealing with assisted reproduction, which is important and relevant here also: 'One response ... is to deny that it is meaningful to talk of the best interests of a potential child, or to compare life in any state, with never existing.' It is clear that under current law, 'potential life' holds no currency and has no rights.

In all cases there is agreement about the value of life; however, the views concerning value of 'potential' life vary.

Mother's versus child's interests, double effect

A crucial area of the abortion debate involves the rights of a woman during pregnancy. The abortion law is clearly geared towards the choice that a woman has over her own body but there are also philosophical and religious considerations.

The theologian and philosopher Aquinas taught that the taking of innocent human life is justifiable if the intention to kill is not the primary concern of the action. This has been demonstrated in cases where a woman has an ectopic pregnancy and removal of the fetus is almost certain to kill it, or in cases where treating the woman for cancer could mean the death of the fetus. The **doctrine of double effect** (see also Chapter 2.2) avoids the obvious questions about which is of greater value or which has the most right to life because it prioritises action based upon what 'ought' to be done and not on the consequences of the action.

The right to life

The underlying question here is the right to life of all those involved. This must include both the established personhood and the woman involved. When the rights of both are in direct conflict, for example when the mother's life is at risk, the law is clear – but is it ethically justified? Several questions remain:

● When rights have been awarded, is it then appropriate to consider the relative importance of different rights?

● Are those of the personhood limited and restricted or basic in any way?

● Does the woman's right to choice supersede the basic right to life of the personhood?

Key quote

'We may take the doctrine of the sanctity of human life to be no more than a way of saying that human life has some very special value … The view that human life has unique value is deeply rooted in our society and is enshrined in our law.'

(Peter Singer)

Doctrine of double effect – the idea that even if a good act results in bad consequences, then it is still right to do that act.

Now test yourself

1 Write down four different views about when life actually begins.

2 Explain the difference between 'sanctity of life' and those views put forward by Peter Singer and science.

3 According to Tony Hope, what does the law state about the value of potential life?

Answers online

Tested

Ethical issues involved in legislation about abortion

Revised

History of British abortion legislation

The history of the law against abortion begins with the Offences Against the Person Act 1861, which depicts procuring a miscarriage as a criminal act. In 1929 the Infant Preservation Act allowed the preservation of the mother's life as reason for a termination.

The politician David Steel introduced the Abortion Act 1967 that stated that two doctors must agree that an abortion is necessary. It is deemed necessary if:

- the woman's physical health is threatened by having the baby
- any existing children would be harmed mentally or physically by the woman proceeding to have the baby
- there is a high risk the baby would be disabled.

This was clarified by the Embryology Act 1990 (section 37):

'... it now states that a person is not guilty of an offence under the law of abortion when termination is performed by a registered practitioner and two registered medical practitioners have formed the opinion in good faith that the continuance of the pregnancy would involve risk, greater than if the pregnancy were terminated, of injury to the physical or mental health of the pregnant woman or any existing children of her family.

(Mason and Laurie)

In addition, the legal limit was reduced from 28 weeks to 24 weeks. The 1990 Act, however, also removed time restrictions for a fetus aborted due to abnormality. The Act determines that an abortion can be performed after 24 weeks only to save the mother.

Ethical issues

There are several ethical issues raised by abortion legislation:

- The conscience of the medical practitioner; doctors may refuse to carry out abortions on grounds of conscientious objection.
- There is a conflict between what is seen as 'sinful' by some people but on the other hand 'lawful'.
- The law is consequential and dependent on establishing reasons to justify actions and yet this is only one of many possible (ethical) approaches.
- Does an abnormal fetus not have the same rights as an ordinary fetus? If so, who decides the extent of abnormality?
- The 1990 Act states 'not exceeded its twenty-fourth week'; however, it is only assumed that this is from the date of the woman's last period – this is not clear.
- The fetus has no right to life under current legislation.
- The father of the fetus has no legal rights under current legislation.
- Perhaps the most disturbing issue has been raised by legal professors Mason and Laurie who point out that aborting an 'abnormal' fetus after 24 weeks raises the question of the gynaecologist's actions: 'there is now an infant who, on any interpretation, is entitled to a birth certificate, and, if necessary, a certificate as to the cause of death'.

Typical mistake

There are many technical words to learn in this unit. Make sure that you do not confuse terms in an examination.

Now test yourself

4 Give an example of 'double effect' in abortion.

5 State two issues involved in the legislation regarding abortion.

Answers online

Tested

Arguments for and against abortion

The complexities of religious views about moral issues

The whole idea of a 'religious view' is misleading. Before looking at some points put forward by religions concerning abortion we should be aware of the following factors:

- Within a religion there is often a variety of viewpoints.
- Beyond and between religions there is a variety of viewpoints.

- The views put forward from within religious traditions are based upon a variety of sources of authority including: sacred texts (and their individual interpretation), traditions and cultures, religious leaders, ethical theories, personal convictions.

To say that there is therefore no clear 'unified response' from within a religion is an understatement. This complexity must be understood.

Christianity, Natural Law and Situation Ethics

The Roman Catholic Church

The Roman Catholic Church believes that abortion is murder, breaking the commandment 'Do not kill'. As God has created and given life, it is only God that can take it away – it is no one else's right. Life is holy, given by God and therefore sacred; this is known as the sanctity of life.

Despite this, the Church accepts that the doctrine of double effect (page 54) could allow an abortion to happen, although this is not the same as agreeing with it; rather it simply recognises that it is a consequence of another primary action.

Not all Roman Catholics agree with what the Church teaches. A few Catholics disagree and put forward arguments against enforcing a total ban on abortion. For example:

- Although Church teaching has for a long time stated that a fetus becomes a person when the egg is fertilised, distinguished theologians such as Augustine and Aquinas said this did not happen until between 40 and 80 days after conception.
- The Church has not declared that its teaching on sexual and reproductive issues is infallible.

The Anglican Church

An alternative view is that taken by the Church of England (Anglican), where there is more open debate about abortion. Some within the Anglican tradition would agree with the Roman Catholic Church's position. Some would follow this guidance absolutely.

> **Key quote**
>
> 'In the light of our conviction that the fetus has the right to live and develop as a member of the human family, we see abortion, the termination of that life by the act of man, as a great moral evil.'
>
> (Church of England Board of Social Responsibility, 1980)

Others believe that in certain circumstances it is the lesser of the two evils, for example if the mother is in danger. In many ways this viewpoint agrees with the 1967 Abortion Act 'that in situations where the continuance of a pregnancy threatens the life of the mother a termination of pregnancy may be justified and that there must be adequate and safe provision in our society for such situations' (Church of England General Synod, 1983).

> **Key quote**
>
> 'The Church of England combines strong opposition to abortion with a recognition that there can be – strictly limited – conditions under which it may be morally preferable to any available alternative.'
>
> (General Synod)

Exam practice answers at **www.therevisionbutton.co.uk/myrevisionnotes**

There are others who believe that they should follow the teachings of Jesus, who taught forgiveness and to not judge others. It could be argued that, using the 1967 Abortion Act criteria, abortion in the long term is the most loving and Christian thing to do if it means more suffering would be created by denying it.

Situation Ethics

Finally, some may use the principles of Christian love and argue that if we truly loved others then we would not apply a law without compassion but simply consider each situation on its own merits and opt for the most loving solution. Such thinking is called 'Situation Ethics' and argues that the most loving thing to do always depends on the situation that a person is in (see Chapter 1.2).

> **Situation Ethics** – a theory of ethics according to which moral rules are not absolutely binding but may be modified in the light of specific situations.

Exam tip

Make sure you refer to at least one religion in your answers to questions on responses to abortion and bear in mind the fact that Christian viewpoints also incorporate Natural Law and Situation Ethics.

Now test yourself   Tested

6   Why is there no 'unified response' from religion when it comes to moral issues?

7   Outline two different responses from any of the religious responses to abortion that you have studied.

Answers online

Typical mistake

Avoid being too vague about religious teachings. For AS assessment, depth of knowledge and understanding is required in answers as well as a greater knowledge of the impact of religious ideas upon the issue.

Euthanasia

The issue of euthanasia is equally as complex as abortion and for similar reasons. The context is the end, as opposed to the beginning, of life, yet some of the principles are the same.

Certainly, the ethical issues identified progress under similar headings.

The first problem to consider involves the technical difficulties surrounding the different definitions and types of euthanasia.

Types of euthanasia   Revised

The meaning of the word derives from the Greek 'eu thanatos', interpretations of which include 'good', 'easy', 'gentle' (eu) and 'death' (thanatos).

The following distinctions are based on the ideas of Tony Hope, Professor for Medical Ethics at the University of Oxford and author of key texts for student doctors, *Medical Ethics, A Very Short Introduction* (page 11) and *Medical Ethics and Law* (page 157).

Euthanasia	One person kills another with intention, or allows another's death, for the other's benefit.
Active euthanasia	One person actions another's death for the other's benefit.
Passive euthanasia	By withholding treatment or taking away vital life-prolonging support, one person allows another to die.
Voluntary euthanasia	The request to die by the person who competently wishes it so.
Non-voluntary euthanasia	A decision to die by a second party on behalf of one who is unable to make that decision.
Involuntary euthanasia	One decides to impose or permit death of another even though death is against the other's wishes.
Suicide	One person intentionally killing him or herself.
Assisted suicide	One person helps another to commit suicide.
Physician-assisted suicide	A qualified physician helps another to commit suicide.

Ethical issues involved in legislation about euthanasia

Having clarified and identified the types of euthanasia, it is important to consider the legal status of euthanasia and again, as with applied ethics in general, to debate the workability of any change in law or viewpoint put forward. In Britain, euthanasia is illegal. In 1961 suicide was decriminalised. Despite this, the Suicide Act 1961 was very explicit that to aid or assist suicide in any way was still a crime. Clearly this has implications for euthanasia.

Life and the quality of life: where does life finish?

Generally, a physical end of life can be determined medically. However, for a person in a **persistent vegetative state (PVS)** there are issues surrounding the death of the consciousness. Such a situation again calls into question the definition of life and even whether a physical definition suffices. This is a key question in the euthanasia debate.

Related to this issue are the philosophical questions about quality of life. Is there a point at which one can conclude that life has lost its value? If so, exactly when should this be and who is going to decide?

Human rights

It is interesting to note that: 'patients have the right to decide how much weight to attach to the benefits, burdens, risks and the overall acceptability of any treatment. They have the right to refuse treatment even where refusal may result in harm to themselves or in their own death, and doctors are legally bound to respect their decision' (General Medical Council).

This refers to those who are dying. They have the right not to prolong their life, by refusing treatment. They do not have the right, however, to hasten an end to their life by administering a different course of medication.

Does this pose a contradiction? If a person refuses treatment to prolong life then have they shortened their life? How, in principle, is this different from shortening life in another way?

Thus, human beings have the legal right to the opportunity to extend life but not to shorten it. Where death is inevitable, human beings can only stave it off and are not allowed to welcome it. (This relates to the idea of double effect, see page 54.)

Persistent vegetative state (PVS) – a state in which bodily processes are maintained but the brain is functioning only at its lowest automatic levels.

Key quote

'It is perverse to seek a sense of ethical purity when this is gained at the expense of the suffering of others.'

(Tony Hope)

Exam practice answers at **www.therevisionbutton.co.uk/myrevisionnotes**

There appears to be an uncomfortable inconsistency here. Consciously refusing treatment, knowing that the consequence is death, is seen as acceptable. Consciously willing medication of which the consequence is also death, only sooner and with less pain, is unacceptable. It is this delicate dilemma – if, indeed, it is one – that is at the very heart of the euthanasia debate: namely, just how far should a person's individual rights extend over their own body, fate and destiny?

This discussion of rights is further complicated when the affected party has lost the capacity to indicate preference, the physical ability to commit suicide, or the ability to reason and make an informed decision regarding treatment.

Practical implications

The issue of medical futility is crucial here. What this means is that it raises a question about the point of continued treatment when there is no reasonable hope of cure or of benefit to the patient.

Medical futility raises two key questions:

- Who is to make the decision about terminating life and how is this decision to be reached?
- Is a law that allows euthanasia on the grounds of medical futility workable? Some countries legislate that, under strict conditions, it is.

Arguments against the introduction of a law that allows euthanasia point to the very real risk of abuse:

- How could such a law be effectively monitored?
- Would it be in the best interests of society as a whole?
- Would it be a workable law?
- Further, does euthanasia go against the Hippocratic Oath?
- Is it interfering with the natural or divinely ordained course of events?

Voluntary euthanasia

Voluntary euthanasia is illegal in most countries. Ludwig Minelli is the founder of the movement known as Dignitas. Based in Zurich, Switzerland, Minelli helps people end their lives in the belief that it is their right to decide when they die. People have travelled from all over the world to receive Minelli's help. Despite this technically being voluntary euthanasia, due to complexities of the legal system, Switzerland only allows assisted suicide. Therefore, the death is videoed to ensure the person actively takes the dose; for those who cannot physically take the dose there is a machine that will do it for them if they press a button.

> **Key quote**
>
> 'When suffering is the result of following an ethical principle then we need to look very carefully at our ethical principle and ask whether we are applying it too inflexibly.'
>
> (Tony Hope)

> **Key quote**
>
> 'The doctor's dilemma is self-evident – is he or she practising truly "good" medicine in keeping alive a **neonate** who will be unable to take a place in society or who will be subject to pain and suffering throughout life?'
>
> (Mason and Laurie)

> **Neonate** – another term for newborn child.

> **Now test yourself**
>
> 8 Identify three different types of euthanasia.
>
> 9 List two human rights issues associated with euthanasia.
>
> 10 Explain one practical problem for a doctor if euthanasia were legalised.
>
> Answers online
>
> Tested ☐

The role of hospices and palliative care

Revised

There are some who would argue that voluntary euthanasia is not the answer when our technology and medical care is so advanced that we can make people more comfortable when dying. There are two aspects of care that make this possible.

Palliative care

This is where medication is used to try to remove or reduce the pain in order to improve the quality of life for the individual during the final stage of life. While it cannot treat the illness in terms of providing a cure, **palliative care** endeavours to keep the patient alive for longer and make their exit from this world a dignified one.

Hospices

A **hospice** is a place of refuge for the dying in that it specialises in palliative care but on a more holistic level. Hospices aim to treat the dying person as an individual in terms of concern for their emotional and/or spiritual well-being and not just providing relief for their physical ailments. In addition they provide support for the family. The ultimate aim, just as with palliative care, is for the patient to have a dignified death.

> **Palliative care** – the use of medication to reduce pain or suffering, as opposed to cure.
>
> **Hospice** – a place of refuge for the dying that provides holistic palliative care.

> **Exam tip**
>
> It is important to be able to describe and explain the key facts relating to ethical ideas. However, it is even more important to be able to discuss the implications and questions raised by the ethical issues with the use of quotes and references and the development of key ideas.

Now test yourself

Tested

11 What does the word 'euthanasia' mean?

12 Match the following to their correct definitions:

(a) Active euthanasia		**(i)**	By withholding treatment or taking away vital life-prolonging support one person allows another to die
(b) Passive euthanasia		**(ii)**	The request to die by the person who competently wishes it so
(c) Voluntary euthanasia		**(iii)**	One person actions another's death for the other's benefit
(d) Non-voluntary euthanasia		**(iv)**	One decides to impose or permit death of another even though death is against the other's wishes
(e) Involuntary euthanasia		**(v)**	A decision to die by a second party on behalf of one who is unable to make that decision

Answers online

Arguments for and against euthanasia

Christianity, Natural Law and Situation Ethics

Revised

● Some Christians would never accept the need for euthanasia as they believe that all life is God-given, and only God should decide when people die (sanctity of life). Euthanasia could be seen to break one of the Ten Commandments 'Do not kill' and so some Christians believe God would not allow euthanasia.

● Jesus healed the sick – he did not let them die. Some Christians believe that as humans have free will, they have a choice between life and death, but to choose death, either by euthanasia or suicide, would be a sin.

The Roman Catholic viewpoint supports all the above teachings, promotes the idea of hospices and invests a lot of time and money into care for those who are dying.

> **Key quote**
>
> 'The Lord God formed the man from the dust of the ground and breathed into his nostrils the breath of life, and man became a living being.'
>
> (Genesis 2:7)

The Church of England supports the law not allowing euthanasia, but would accept that in some circumstances to show the greatest love would be to allow someone to die with dignity, and put an end to futile suffering.

Situation Ethics

Other Christians (fewer and mainly thinkers from the more liberal Protestant tradition) would uphold the New Testament teaching that actions should be guided by Christian love. Situation Ethics would argue that it is not Christian to allow pain and suffering needlessly. Every situation should be considered with Christian love (agape).

Typical mistake

When discussing religious ideas, do not assume that all religious believers have the same viewpoint or that they refer to the same source of authority.

Now test yourself

Tested ☐

13 Outline two different responses from any of the religious responses to euthanasia that you have studied.

14 Which religious tradition uses the ethical theories of Natural Law and Situation Ethics?

Answers online

Issues arising

Does the definition of human life stop abortion being murder?

Revised ☐

The definition of human life according to law is that it commences at birth. Clearly this is in conflict with many religious and philosophical views. Scientific views of human life begin much earlier than birth, and so it depends which definition is used. The main issue is when human life is given the status of personhood (see page 32).

Arguments in support of and against the idea that abortion is not murder

In support	Against
A fetus has no legal rights so abortion cannot be murder.	Just because something is 'lawful' does not mean it is not sinful or unjust.
Abortion is in accordance with the Abortion Act and within the law.	Many religious believers see abortion as 'murder' due to definitions of when life begins, i.e. pre-birth.
Cases of double effect mean that even for those religious people who class a fetus as a person the act of abortion is not 'murder'.	Scientific views support the 'potential' arguments used by religious believers.
Some would argue that aborting the fetus is not murder if it means the life of the mother is saved.	

Exam tip

Make a list of the key questions that you could ask in response to this issue. Use this list for your evaluation answers.

Typical mistake

Make sure that you evaluate in your AO2 answers and avoid simply listing or repeating factual information.

Can abortion and euthanasia ever be 'good'?

Revised

The issues of abortion and euthanasia are complex. One of the most common misunderstandings is the view that an argument in support of abortion or an argument against euthanasia equates to seeing the acts of abortion and euthanasia as 'good' *per se*. This is not necessarily the case and depends on many different factors.

Arguments in support of and against the idea that abortion and euthanasia can be 'good'

In support	Against
All depends upon the context and perspective.	Religious and philosophical principles are important here.
Abortion	
Abortion is good because it recognises the rights of a woman, it can save lives and, in cases of rape, can be seen to be part of justice.	Abortion is against the rule 'Do not kill' and so is not good.
It follows the law and so cannot be bad.	It does not recognise God-given life in the womb and so is not good.
Euthanasia	
What 'type' of euthanasia is a factor that determines whether euthanasia is good or not.	It is against religious principles, e.g. God gives and takes life.
Surely something that relieves pain and suffering cannot be described as bad?	It is against the law and is both a sin and a crime.
Euthanasia is good because it brings 'happiness' to those who wish for it.	

Exam tip

Do not just give a list of criticisms like a shopping list. It is far better to discuss and develop three or four criticisms, explaining and responding to them, than to give a list of seven or eight. This demonstrates a process of reasoning and a sustained argument.

Do human beings have a right to life?

Revised

There are various religious and philosophical teachings that support the right to life. In addition, the right to life is a universal human right. Despite this, in the context of abortion, the issue is that the fetus does not have the same rights in law as a religious believer may afford to it. In euthanasia, a right to life does not necessarily mean enforcement.

Arguments in support of and against a human's right to life

In support	Against
The sanctity-of-life teaching explores two aspects – life is precious, a gift and so should be cherished but also that it is God's decision when that life begins and ends.	The fetus is not considered as having the right to life and so the argument is not relevant for abortion.
Religion is life-affirming and not defeatist – abortion and euthanasia contradict this principle.	Likewise a person in a PVS or on life support may not be classed as independently alive and so euthanasia is not taking life away.
Life begins at conception because the resulting product of conception is already a *homo sapiens* with the potential to develop.	A right to life does not necessarily mean that one is forced to keep it – the right to life involves the right to decide as integral.

Typical mistake

Some candidates use quotations that are not always relevant to their argument. Be careful when using quotes in critical assessments.

Exam tip

Always make sure that quotations relate to the argument you are presenting. To make sure of this, always explain the relevance of the quote in your answer.

Do human beings have a right to choose to die?

Revised

One of the basic human rights is the right to choose – the freedom to decide the course of one's life. However, when the impact of that decision affects others or causes danger, this right needs suspending for the common good. It is this debate that is relevant here.

In support	Against
Individuals are allowed personal convictions and should not have other ideologies imposed upon them; therefore people should be able to do as they wish.	Euthanasia is illegal – we have responsibility to choose good and legal actions.
It is not only rational to allow someone who is suffering to die, it is also compassionate.	A person may not be of sound mind and arguments may be emotive and clouded by irrational points based upon context and subjectivity.
People can make rational decisions through directives stated in wills that are set out clearly in advance and this will demonstrate that they were of sound mind in making this decision and are not making it emotively in response to the situation.	There are hospices, and the palliative care of the NHS is highly regarded as a legal and compassionate alternative and so supports the rights of individuals in a different way.
The role of Dignitas in promoting human rights and freedom to choose.	The issue of euthanasia is not an individual one because it affects society as a whole.
Subjectivity – a person's own life experience should be sufficient enough for him or her to evidence why he or she is making the decision.	

Exam practice

(a) Explain the different ideas concerning the start of human life.

(30 marks)

(b) 'Abortion cannot be considered murder.' Consider how far this is true.

(15 marks)

Answers online

Online

Exam tip

It is essential that you make a list of questions to ask in response to your studies. For every quote, piece of evidence, proposal or argument, try to think of a counter argument that is relevant.

Now test yourself

15 State two different viewpoints in response to whether or not abortion is 'murder'.

16 Give two examples of when abortion can be said to be 'good'.

17 Give two examples of when abortion cannot be said to be 'good'.

18 State two different viewpoints in response to whether or not euthanasia is 'murder'.

19 Give two examples of where euthanasia can be said to be 'good'.

20 Give two examples of where euthanasia cannot be said to be 'good'.

Answers online

Tested

2.1 Kant's theory of ethics

Kant's ethical theory

The deontological approach
Revised

According to the philosopher Kant, moral value is not judged by the consequences of the act but by the actual act itself. Thus Kant has a **deontological** approach to ethics. If a certain act is right, then it is right in all circumstances and in all conditions. Kant also believed that we are obligated to act morally and so obey the moral law.

> **Deontological** – a term used to denote an ethical theory that is based upon the belief that an action is intrinsically wrong or right, irrespective of consequences.

Reason and morality
Revised

Kant argued that there was an objective **moral law** and that knowledge of this law could be gained through reason. This approach was typical of the **Enlightenment** period of philosophy (eighteenth-century Europe), which was known as the 'age of reason' and in which reason was the touchstone by which everything else was judged.

Kant argued that human beings are rational and so are able to work out what is right and wrong. The actions that emanate from the rational moral law are either morally right or wrong in themselves, that is, intrinsically good or bad. Kant also believed that moral laws were binding on human beings. This stemmed from his views about human beings as rational beings.

> **Moral law** – Kant's idea of an eternal, unchanging moral system.
>
> **Enlightenment** – the period of philosophy in the eighteenth century renowned for its emphasis on reason.

Good will

Kant's ideas are formulated in the *Critique of Practical Reason* and begin with the idea of good will. When we are driven by a desire to act to always do right, i.e. to do one's duty, then we are said to act with a good will. Good will is the highest form of good. This is because it is not concerned about consequences or self-interest. When we act with a good will, then we act with the intention of being moral. The key element is the intention behind the act.

Kant distinguished between behaviour and intention. It is the inner motive that is the vital element, since outward behaviour, however good it seems, does not necessarily reveal a good will. A good will is the one that does the right thing with the right intention.

In opposition to **teleological** ethics, practical reason focuses on the development of a good will and not on the achievement of happiness. Through this, reason can deduce maxims (principles) for behaviour that are universally applicable. This idea of a maxim is the imperative or duty to act in a certain way.

> **Key quote**
>
> 'Two things fill the mind with ever new and increasing admiration and awe … the starry heavens above me and the moral law within me.'
>
> (Immanuel Kant)

> **Key quote**
>
> 'It is impossible to conceive of anything at all in the world … which can be taken as good without qualification, except a good will.'
>
> (Immanuel Kant)

> **Teleological** – an ethical theory that considers the consequences of a particular action, or the 'end' result, and it is the assessment of this 'end' that determines whether or not the action is morally good.

Contrast with teleological approaches

An imperative is something that must be done. The **hypothetical imperative** informs us of a factual relation between a particular goal and how to achieve it. In terms of ethics, teleological approaches use goals such as happiness (**Utilitarianism**). There is no concept of obligation or duty attached to such an approach. Kant did not see this type of imperative as referring to morality. For Kant, morality was not about achieving goals; morality was an end in itself. Morality was about **categorical imperatives** which have intrinsic authority. Categorical imperatives are the absolute maxims and demand unconditional obedience based on duty: 'if the action is represented as good in itself … then the imperative is categorical', argues Kant.

> **Hypothetical imperative** – an action is considered as right depending upon a condition and usually takes the form of 'if … then it is right'.
>
> **Utilitarianism** – ethical theory that argues that the correct way of action is that derived from working out what brings happiness to the greatest number. See page 8.
>
> **Categorical imperative** – Kant's idea that an action is intrinsically right irrespective of context or consequence.

Now test yourself

1 What is meant by the term 'Enlightenment period of philosophy'?
2 Write down two things Kant states about moral laws.
3 What is good will?
4 Explain the difference between deontological and teleological.
5 What is a 'categorical imperative'?

Answers online

Typical mistake

Make sure that you can clearly explain the difference between the technical terms and do not get them confused with each other.

Exam tip

Kant's ideas are very difficult to express. Try separating the key elements of his thought – reason, good will, categorical imperative – and writing your own explanations on revision cards. This will help you explain things better in an examination situation.

The importance of duty

Since it is not the consequences of our acts that confer moral value on them (teleological approach), it is our duty to act morally according to the categorical imperatives that have intrinsic moral worth (deontological approach) and as such establish our parameters of behavior through universal maxims. Therefore duty is a universal obligation and conveys willing obedience to universal maxims and the laws derived from these. Duty, then, is clearly linked to good will, which in turn is the highest good.

Kant believed that when we act out of duty, we are acting out of a desire to be moral. Kant also made clear that it is not our duty to do things that we are unable to do. The 'ought' of moral actions is only applicable when it implies 'can'. In other words, it is only meaningful to say I 'ought' to do something, if, in fact, I 'can' do it.

Kant also argued that the will is free and independent. This is necessary for morality to be meaningful. To make rational choices we must be free, and to do our duty we must be free. If our actions are not the result of free choices, then our actions cannot be regarded as the acts of a moral agent.

The categorical imperative

Kant held that the 'categories' by which we understand the world – categories like space, time and causality – were *not* derived from experience. Rather the mind imposes categories on all its experiences (for example, we cannot prove anything has a cause; we assume it and confirm by experience). Thus Kant argued that we cannot prove that we ought to do something by analysing it, since we will never have enough evidence. For Kant, the idea of moral obligation comes from within ourselves – and we experience it as the 'categorical imperative'.

In contrast to the hypothetical imperative, the categorical imperative has a binding force on people, irrespective of their interests. Kant saw moral principles as commands that are true and, as such, they are obligatory. Kant devised various formulations of the categorical imperative which act as general rules to gauge whether an act is moral. Three of these are as follows:

1. Universal law

Kant argued that the only actions that are moral are those actions that can be universalised (i.e. applied in all situations and to all rational beings, without exception).

2. Treat human beings as ends not as means to an end

Kant held human beings as the pinnacle of creation. Therefore, it can never be moral to exploit people, to use them as a means to an end. Each person is unique and of equal value and so cannot be sacrificed, even if it would result in some overall greater good.

3. Act on the assumption that all will act in the same way

Kant argued that our actions had to be based on the assumption that others would also act morally and treat everyone as ends, not means.

> **Key quote**
>
> 'Act only according to that maxim by which you can at the same time, will that it should become a universal law.'
>
> (Immanuel Kant)
>
> 'So act that you treat humanity, both in your own person and in the person of every other human being, never merely as a means, but always at the same time as an end.'
>
> (Immanuel Kant)
>
> 'So act as if you were through your maxim a law-making member of a kingdom of ends.'
>
> (Immanuel Kant)

> **Now test yourself**
>
> 6 What is duty?
> 7 What did Kant mean by the words 'ought' and 'can'?
> 8 What are the three maxims of the categorical imperative?
>
> Answers online
>
> Tested

The *summum bonum*

Kant referred to the highest good as the ***summum bonum***. The highest good was the best possible good and he saw this as comprising of virtue and happiness. Kant was aware that the basic ideas behind his ethical system are 'postulates', by which he meant things we assume or take for granted as being the case. Kant identified three **postulates** for his ethical system: freedom, immortality and the existence of God.

He argued that:

- Our moral experience shows that we are under an obligation to achieve goodness or virtue, and not merely an 'average' level of morality but the highest standard possible. If we recognise the 'ought' and the 'can', then we must also postulate freedom to act according to our duty because morality without freedom would be illogical.

- Beyond this, we recognise also that true virtue should be rewarded by happiness, for it would not be a rationally satisfying state of affairs if happiness came to the unvirtuous or unhappiness to the virtuous. If people were virtuous but were also in pain and misery, their virtue would still be valuable but, nevertheless, the total situation would not be the best possible.

- The desired state of affairs in which human beings are both virtuous and happy is called by Kant the '*summum bonum*' (highest good). This we recognise to be what ought to happen.

> ***Summum bonum*** – highest good where virtue and happiness meet.
>
> **Postulate** – assumption or something taken for granted.

> **Typical mistake**
>
> Candidates often get confused when explaining the *summum bonum*. To avoid confusion, clearly identify and number the stages of the argument. When you have explained the argument, use a different colour pen to identify the three postulates.

Exam practice answers at **www.therevisionbutton.co.uk/myrevisionnotes**

- Now, in Kant's famous argument, 'ought' implies 'can'. This means that an obligation to achieve something implies the possibility that the goal can be achieved (otherwise there can be no obligation). It has to be possible, therefore, for the *summum bonum* to be achieved.

- However, while humans can achieve virtue, it is outside their power to ensure that virtue is rewarded or coincides with happiness. Such proportioning clearly does not take place before death, so Kant also argued that there must be survival after death. The *summum bonum* must therefore be achieved in a different life or world and so supposes the existence of life after death (immortality).

- Thus there also is a need to postulate the existence of God as the one who has the power to bring virtue and happiness into harmony in that next life. This is the only way that fairness will be achieved in the universe with virtue and happiness harmonised.

Note that Kant was not arguing that morality is invalid if God's existence is denied. For Kant, the fact that something is a duty or obligation is sufficient reason to do it. However, he thought that God was demanded if the goal of morality was to be realised.

Now test yourself

9   What is the *summum bonum*?

10 What are Kant's three postulates for the *summum bonum*?

Answers online

Tested

Exam tip

Make sure that you focus on the question. If the question is on the *summum bonum*, do not write an answer that explains all about Kant's ethical theory as some of your answer will be irrelevant.

Application to an ethical issue

Approach ——————————————————————— Revised

When applying Kant's ethical system to ethical issues it is important to identify the key ideas behind his theory, such as reason, duty, good will and the identification of a universal moral law. However, it is the two maxims of the categorical imperative – universalisation and means to an end – that assist us in considering what a Kantian approach could be.

Abortion ——————————————————————— Revised

In general, Kantian ethics argues against abortion on the grounds that we have a duty to preserve life. It does raise questions about the status of the **fetus** and the timing of the abortion. However, it could be argued that whatever the status, the fetus develops into a rational free human being. It is unlikely that the developed human being would later support the view that he or she should have been aborted rather than allowed to develop.

Universal law

The universalisation of the rule that everyone should not have an abortion is clearly acceptable. One good reason is because if everyone did have an abortion the human race would become extinct! It might be possible to reformulate by limiting it to when the woman's life is in danger.

Another reformulation might concern the future mental state of the developed fetus. Some Kantians might argue that if the mental state was so limited that the person would be unable to reason or make choices, then abortion could be seen as permissible. This could be argued on the grounds that the fetus and the resulting human being had no intrinsic value.

Fetus – the unborn baby from the end of the eighth week after conception (when the major structures have formed) until birth.

Typical mistake

Candidates sometimes tend to drift away from Kant's specific maxims and contrast with other approaches that then lead to digression into irrelevant material.

Now test yourself

11 What are the key elements behind Kant's ethical theory?

12 Which maxims from Kant's idea of the categorical imperative can be applied effectively to moral issues?

Answers online

Tested

Treat human beings as ends not as means to an end

If the fetus is regarded as a person, then an abortion would mean that the person was treated as a means rather than an end. In other words, the fetus (person) was exploited. It was used (destroyed) to benefit the mother.

Issues arising

Kant's ethical theory raises issues about the strengths and weaknesses of deontological ethics but also raises other issues specific to Kant's ideology, such as the view of a human as a rational being and also the goal of the *summum bonum*.

> **Exam tip**
>
> If you are asked about Kant's application to an issue, keep it clearly focused. Simply identify your issue and explain what maxims would apply and the impact they would have on application. Do not spend too long explaining the theory.

Can reason be the basis of a successful ethical system?

Revised

Kant's theory is based in reason, as was typical of Enlightenment thought. However, the wisdom of such an approach has been questioned regarding its relevance to ethics.

In support	Against
Reason is used in all ethical systems. You cannot identify the best result for ethical decisions without first working out some form of success criteria.	Reason is almost abstract from the human condition and cannot account for how people 'feel' about things.
The most influential ethical system within the history of Christianity – that of **natural moral law** – is grounded in reason and recognised by the Church as being consistent and fair.	Applying reason to actions has led many to argue for self-interest as a motive.
The use of reasoning as a basis avoids being guided by emotion.	Since human behaviour is directly related to emotions, some (e.g. the philosopher Ayer) have argued that ethics should be about emotions and not reason.
Kant argued that desires and emotions are not good guides because they result in inequality and unfairness in ethics.	The use of reason alone and the application of absolutes invite criticisms of a deontological system, e.g. it is too inflexible, lacks compassion and is contradictory in practice.
	The idea of universal principles derived through reason assumes that everyone has the same sense of duty and does not recognise different cultural perceptions of right and wrong.

> **Natural moral law** – the idea that the natural world dictates a moral order discoverable through reason.

> **Exam tip**
>
> For AO2, try to create a balanced argument by considering both sides and alternative views of different ideas from different sources.

Exam practice answers at **www.therevisionbutton.co.uk/myrevisionnotes**

Strengths and weaknesses of Kantian ethics

Revised

Strengths	Weaknesses
It states clear rules. For instance, it is generally against abortion on the grounds that we have a duty to preserve life, and whatever the status of the fetus, it will develop into a rational human being.	Kant put 'obligation' as the reason for acting morally. However, it is not clear why that motive is superior to motives such as love and compassion. Many may feel that it is difficult to defend keeping someone alive on the grounds of 'obligation', when that person is suffering acutely with terminal illness. The appeal to love and compassion, which sound like higher motives, seems ignored.
It emphasises the importance of each person. Everyone is equally valued in their own right.	Fundamental to Kant's theory is the idea of being free to choose as an individual and the notion that humans are rational beings. However, both of these have been challenged. Modern science looks to nurture and nature to explain the cause of our actions, while experience of life seems to suggest that people do not always act rationally.
It is applied universally and is therefore impartial. If a certain act is right, then it is right in all circumstances.	Kant claimed that there was only one categorical imperative and the other maxims were just stating the same point in a different way. However, it is disputed whether the three aspects of the categorical imperative are equivalent, meaning that Kant's system is incoherent.
It treats people as ends rather than means to an end. Therefore it is against exploitation of people. This approach gives high value to human beings.	It does not accept exceptions and so is not flexible enough. What happens if two duties conflict? For instance, the duty to preserve life can conflict with the duty to protect life, as in the case of war.
It emphasises motive and intention rather than just the outward behaviour. This avoids the problem of doing something that appears outwardly good, but is, in fact, carried out for immoral reasons. In such a case, Kantian ethics would deem such an act immoral.	Is universalisability feasible? The deontological approach does not allow for the variety of situations that arise.
	Why make the assumption that only God can bring about the highest good?
	Why make the assumption that virtue must be rewarded with happiness?
	Sense of duty can be explained by other means, for example how we are moulded by society.

Typical mistake

Candidates sometimes write a shopping list of reasons for and against an argument without really engaging with the materials themselves. Make sure you explain every point clearly before moving on to another.

Exam tip

Try drawing a clear conclusion with reasons or, for a high-level answer, make sure that you are evaluating throughout your answer and demonstrating a clear process of reasoning.

How coherent is Kant's idea of *summum bonum*?

Revised

Coherent	Incoherent
It is based in reason and so is easy to follow and apply.	Some may say that the idea of pure reason in itself is incoherent with the nature of ethics that encompasses emotions and sometimes serious clashes of ideals causing irresolvable dilemmas.
Clear guidance results from application of maxims – the idea of universal rules.	Ethics deals with 'messy' and complex situations; the Kantian approach, albeit sophisticated in origin, is far too simplistic in practice.
It focuses on the individual as central to ethics and not as a means to an end.	In this way, it is also inflexible and not conducive to ethical matters.
It is based in three postulates (freedom, immortality and the existence of God) which ultimately provide the coherence to the theory.	It could be accused of being inhumane and lacking compassion, which is inconsistent with the idea of pursuing virtue.
	Its deontological origins are open to all the usual criticisms, for example it is too inflexible, lacks compassion and is contradictory in practice.
	Since human moral decision making is based upon freedom and an autonomous law, there does not need to be a God figure for morality to 'work' and yet Kant's *summum bonum* contradicts this by postulating a God to make sense of his ethical system.

Are Kant's ideas about human beings realistic?

Revised

Kant's ideas about human beings

Kant's writings stress that human beings occupy a special place in creation. Humans are different from all other creatures, and not just different but superior. Kant believed that human beings have an intrinsic worth or dignity which makes them valuable 'above all price'. Animals do not have this.	So humans are unique among all species within the universe. Human uniqueness is based in humanity's ability to be rational agents – free agents who have the ability to make decisions and guide their actions through reason. If there were no rational beings, the moral dimension of the world would no longer exist.

Realistic	Unrealistic
Optimistic ability to reason – this is what distinguishes human beings from other species according to the views of many people.	Not all human beings have the same level of reason to work out duty.
The key ideas are realistic – duty and deontology (the idea that we have clear, set rules for behaviour).	If philosophers have to work it out for others, how can it be a true categorical? For example, if a categorical imperative is a universal sense of duty then why do we have to work it out?
Universality of morality in core issues, for example issues of life and death, seems fair.	Morality is not universally the same and varies from culture to culture and also from age to age.

Exam tip

For revision, try writing a list of key questions for each area of the issues arising in the specification.

Typical mistake

Timing: make sure that you leave enough time to write your answers for the (b) questions. Some candidates run out of time and lose quite a few marks.

How compatible are these aspects of Kant's ethics with a religious approach to ethics?

Revised

Compatible	Incompatible
The idea that a moral law is given by God supports the idea of moral absolutes.	They are in stark contrast to teleological, consequential systems such as **Situation Ethics.**
Some Christians would indicate that the Ten Commandments are clear examples of categorical imperatives at work.	The inflexibility of an absolutist system is inconsistent with the ideas of forgiveness, tolerance and non-judgement.
There are clear parallels with natural moral law (see page 51), especially the idea of reason.	If a system is therefore inflexible its application can appear to be lacking virtue and thus clearly inconsistent with virtuous religious teaching.
The *summum bonum* is clearly a religious concept when one identifies the postulates of practical reason, and Kant himself was openly religious.	Kant's system can be totally independent of God as human beings make their own decisions and the law is autonomous and independent of religion.
The idea of virtue and reward is the basis of religious morality; for example, heaven and hell, the idea of judgement.	

Situation Ethics – a theory of ethics according to which moral rules are not absolutely binding but may be modified in the light of specific situations.

Now test yourself

Tested

13 What are the key areas to consider in evaluating Kant's ethical theories?

14 Give an example of how the idea of the *summum bonum* is coherent as a concept.

15 List two ways Kant's theory is compatible with religion.

16 Outline two weaknesses of Kant's ethical theory.

Answers online

Exam practice

(a) Explain Kant's idea of the *summum bonum* in relation to his theory of ethics. **(30 marks)**

(b) 'Kant's theory of ethics is completely incompatible with a religious approach to ethics.' Assess this claim. **(15 marks)**

Answers online

Online

2.2 Natural Law and ethics

What is Natural Law?

Natural Law is based on a particular view about nature and the universe. That view is that the universe has a natural order that works to achieve an 'end' or 'purpose'. This order, direction or purpose is determined by a supernatural power. Human beings are part of the natural world and so they too have a 'purpose' or 'nature'. It is a nature that is in all human beings. Natural Law is therefore about acting in such ways that we consistently move towards this 'purpose'. Some argue that the ideals behind Natural Law can be traced back to ancient philosophers such as Aristotle.

> **Key quote**
>
> 'The idea of natural law is sometimes described as the view that there is an unchanging, normative order that is part of the natural world.'
>
> (Stephen Buckle, philosopher)

Aristotle's four causes — Revised

Aristotle (384–322BCE) reasoned that there were four causes that lay behind everything. These causes answer the question, 'What makes something what it "is"?'

Cause	Definition
Material cause	What the object is made of. For example, a statue could be made of bronze though the bronze in itself does not make the statue what it is.
Formal cause	What determines the object and makes it be what it is. For example, some idea that the sculptor has in mind when fashioning the statue.
Efficient cause	What makes the thing that is caused. For example, the fashioning of the bronze by the artist.
Final cause	Why the thing has been made. For example, the statue was made to commemorate something.

These four causes are clearly identified in man-made objects, but what about natural objects?

Explaining man-made and natural objects — Revised

Aristotle developed his thinking into explaining the final cause for living things as well, that is, their purpose. It is not obvious what the final cause of a natural object is. The final cause of a non-living object such as a statue must have been in the mind of the artist (external to it). The case of a living object is different. Aristotle sees the final cause in terms of the function it performs. Objects in nature seemed to be driven towards a goal to obtain a certain form proper to them, and their actions are all directed towards this goal. Aristotle refers to this goal as '**telos**'.

> **Telos** – the end or purpose of something or its function; for Aristotle, the telos of a human being was to be rational and moral.

Aristotle thought the **teleological** goal for man was to live a life of a certain kind, that is, to be a reasoning creature and to use reason to recognise how to behave (i.e. morally). It is when human beings act morally that their purpose of telos is fulfilled. Hence the combination of reason and moral action is in accordance with the natural order of things.

Overall, Aristotle saw the goal (purpose) of human life as **'eudaimonia'** (happiness). He argued that we pursue other goals in order ultimately to achieve happiness. Confusion can arise because of modern usage of the word 'happiness'. For Aristotle, 'happiness' was very different from 'pleasure' since he regarded the pursuit of pleasure for its own sake as mere gratification. In contrast, happiness was living well and being fulfilled, since it involved behaving rationally (i.e. consistently with human nature and the order of the natural world). Therefore, he thought that making reasoned choices would lead to happiness. In this thinking, we can see the germination of classical Natural Law.

> **Teleological** – an ethical theory that considers the consequences of a particular action, or the 'end' result, and it is the assessment of this 'end' that determines whether or not the action is morally good.
>
> **Eudaimonia** – a term used by Aristotle literally meaning 'good spirit' and is translated as 'happiness' or 'well-being'.

Now test yourself

Tested ▢

1. Match up the correct causes with their definitions:
   - **(a)** Efficient
   - **(b)** Formal
   - **(c)** Final
   - **(d)** Material
   - **(i)** its purpose
   - **(ii)** what produced it
   - **(iii)** what it consists of
   - **(iv)** what it is
2. How does Aristotle link purpose to ethics?

Answers online

> **Key quote**
>
> 'From the beginning natural law theories drew on disparate elements, which, waxing and waning at different times, shaped and reshaped the doctrine accordingly.'
>
> (Stephen Buckle)

> **Exam tip**
>
> When asked about the four causes, make sure that you clearly link your answer to ethics.

> **Typical mistake**
>
> Do not include too much biographical information about thinkers at the expense of digressing from the question.

Aquinas' development

It is with the Roman lawyer, Cicero, where the account of a natural law made its first systematic appearance:

> **True law is right reason in agreement with nature; it is of universal application, unchanging and everlasting; it summons to duty by its commands, and averts from wrongdoings by its prohibitions.**

For Cicero, the 'author' of this law was God. This connection between Natural Law and an eternal or divine law was developed by the medieval theologian and philosopher Thomas Aquinas.

The idea of natural good

Revised ▢

For Aquinas, the natural law was located in the activity of human reasoning. By applying reason to moral problems, we will find that we act consistently with the natural law. Such acts are deemed good acts, or **natural good**, since they are in line with our true human nature and purpose. For Aquinas, the natural law was created by God and designed to achieve the ultimate purpose – to enjoy fellowship with God, to be perfect in the image of God. For Aquinas, obeying Natural Law meant carrying out actions that develop our image to reflect the image of God more closely.

> **Natural good** – the idea of a universal recognition of what is good.

Reasoning wrongly

This idea that there is a universal natural standard of good needed to be worked out. Natural law is within all of us but it is not like a physical law that has to be followed. It derives from reason and reason can sometimes be in error. Aquinas recognised that sometimes we do not do the things that we should. We reason wrongly.

One example of reasoning wrongly would be if a good was pursued that actually was not a good as understood by Natural Law (i.e. it did not develop perfection). It is what is referred to as 'an apparent good'. For example, applying compassion to someone who requests to end their life (euthanasia, see Chapter 1.4) may seem a good thing to do but is not in the natural order of things according to Natural Law. Aquinas argued that our sinful nature can lead us astray to choose things that we desire but which may not be contributing to our development into the image of God.

Developing correct reasoning

One way that correct reasoning can be developed is through the cultivation of certain virtues. Natural virtues are:

- prudence
- temperance
- fortitude
- justice.

Theological virtues (revealed by the Bible) are:

- faith
- hope
- charity.

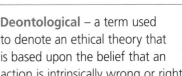

Now test yourself

3 Why is Cicero important to Natural Law?

4 List two of Aquinas' theological virtues.

5 Name two of Aquinas' natural virtues.

Answers online

Tested ☐

Natural Law ethics ──────────────────────── Revised ☐

Natural Law ethics involves using reason to work out the morally correct behaviour that is in accordance with the goal of being human. It is usually regarded as being **deontological** and absolutist:

- deontological because what should be done is seen as being determined by fundamental principles that are not based on consequences
- absolutist because it identifies the right action by means of the **primary precepts** (see below).

Aquinas gave Natural Law a religious interpretation; however, for Aquinas, although God was the author of the natural order, reason still played a key role in his development of Natural Law. God was seen as the source of the natural law, which was rooted in the human mind. Aquinas also saw God as having designed us for perfection. He believed that we were made in God's image and our purpose was to reflect perfectly this image.

Aquinas did not think that this perfection could be discovered by Natural Law alone because the purpose of being human is eternal and not temporal.

> **Deontological** – a term used to denote an ethical theory that is based upon the belief that an action is intrinsically wrong or right, irrespective of consequences.
>
> **Primary precepts** – established principles of behaviour from which guidance and application can be sought for ethical reasoning.

The divine or eternal law we only know in part since it refers to the principles by which God governs the universe.

- Divine law refers to the Bible, which guides us in reaching our goal of perfection by the teachings it contains. However, Aquinas believed that such perfection was not achievable in this life, but only after death.
- Natural Law for Aquinas, then, is the part of this eternal, divine law that applies to human choices and can be known by our natural reason.

Now test yourself

6 What is Natural Law ethics?
7 What is 'divine law'?
8 According to Aquinas, how does Natural Law ethics relate to the divine law?

Answers online

Tested

Principle of double effect

Revised

Aquinas made a distinction between the intention of an act and the act itself. For those looking on, it may well be judged that an action was good. However, if the onlooker knew the real motive or intention, then it may well be seen rather differently. Likewise it is not acceptable to do a bad act intentionally even if the aim is to bring about good outcomes.

This approach to understanding intentions is important when applying Natural Law to moral dilemmas. It is at the heart of what is known as the '**doctrine of double effect**'. This states that even if a good act results in bad consequences, then it is still right to do that act. It is still right to do that act, even if it was known that bad consequences would result. The important issue is the intention. If the intention was not to bring about these bad consequences, then the unfortunate side effects do not make the act morally wrong.

> **Doctrine of double effect** – the idea that even if a good act results in bad consequences, then it is still right to do that act.

Classical formulations of the principle of double effect require that four conditions be met if the action is to be morally permissible:

- that we do not wish the evil effects, and make all reasonable efforts to avoid them
- that the immediate effect be good in itself
- that the evil is not made a means to obtain the good effect
- that the good effect be as important (proportionate) at least as the evil effect.

An example of this would be treating a pregnant woman for cancer in order to save her life but at the same time destroying the unborn child. Since the death of the unborn child was not the intention of the act that produced it but rather an unfortunate side effect, then the act that brought it about is deemed good and morally right, according to Natural Law ethics.

> **Exam tip**
> Make sure you use all your technical terms correctly, for example natural good, double effect, etc.

Casuistry

What is casuistry?

Revised

The word 'casuistry' originates from the Latin word 'casus', meaning 'case'. Casuistry is when core principles of predetermined moral behaviour are applied to a 'case', context or situation. Reason is used to apply the rule and determine judgement on the morality of the situation. This is not,

> **Key quote**
> 'Casuistry is the science of judging cases of conscience, or moral problems.'
> (Peter Holmes, philosopher)

however, a teleological approach due to the predetermined absolute principles that are brought to the case.

For Aquinas, his idea of casuistry involved the application of what he called primary precepts to work out secondary precepts which were then used as a guide for moral situations.

Natural Law in action
Revised

Primary precepts

The primary precepts apply to all human beings without exception. They are good acts because they lead us towards the main human purpose or goal. The most fundamental one that underpins them all is: 'Act in such a way as to achieve good and avoid evil'.

This summary identifies the most basic natural inclination. From this, Aquinas then identified five more general inclinations or tendencies. In one sense they can be seen as fundamental principles that must be followed in order to achieve the required ends. These five principles are as follows:

- Preserve innocent life.
- Live in an orderly manner in society.
- Worship God.
- Educate children.
- Reproduce to continue the species.

Secondary precepts

From these primary precepts, secondary ones can be deduced. The difference between the primary and secondary is that the primary precepts are always true and held universally, without exception. They are also self-evident. In contrast, the secondary precepts are not strictly universal since they may not hold in certain circumstances. They are also derived from reasoning from the primary precepts.

An example of a secondary precept would be 'Do not steal'. This reflects the primary precept of 'orderly living in society'. However, it is accepted that sometimes situations occur whereby not following secondary precepts may be supported by another primary precept. For example, if the act of stealing was for the purpose of feeding a hungry child, then the primary precept of preserving innocent life takes precedence. In such a case the act is justified. Natural Law always demands that a primary precept is adhered to. It is this sort of 'working out' that is casuistry.

The theologian Ronald Preston thought that the flaw with casuistry was with those who made use of casuistry; i.e. that it lay with those who applied it, and not with the discipline of casuistry itself. Indeed, he maintains that casuistry is essential: it involves the careful use of thought in applying general principles to particular circumstances: 'Christian ethics would be an exercise in ignorance without it'.

> **Exam tip**
>
> When answering a question on Natural Law, make sure that you focus on the area highlighted in the question. Make sure you pick out the key points and explain why they are important in relation to the question. Ensuring a focus on the question means that 'information is mostly accurate and relevant' (AO1).

> **Typical mistake**
>
> It is good to prepare and practise answers; however, do not simply repeat a prepared answer but instead use the information in it to answer the question that is set on the paper. Always stay focused on the question asked.

> **Now test yourself**
>
> 9 What is casuistry?
> 10 Name Aquinas' primary precepts.
>
> Answers online
>
> Tested

A modern development

Finnis and practical reason

John Finnis, professor of law and philosophy, makes a modern statement for Natural Law in his famous book *Natural Law and Natural Rights* published in 1980. In this book, Finnis develops the idea of the primary precepts of Aquinas and gives them a more modern feel. Once again, coming back to the idea of a natural good, first identified by Aristotle somewhat vaguely in his concept of 'eudaimonia' (happiness) and then developed by Aquinas into natural good, Finnis uses the term 'well-being' to establish what the telos, end or purpose for humanity ideally is.

Like Aquinas and others, Finnis stresses the importance of reasoning: 'From one's capacity to grasp intelligently the basic forms of good as "to-be-pursued", one gets one's ability ... to sympathetically (though not uncritically) see the point of actions, life-styles, characters and cultures that one would not choose for oneself.'

Basic forms of good

In using reason, human beings can identify what Finnis calls basic values or 'basic forms of good'. He identifies seven of these:

1 Life

2 Knowledge

3 Play

4 Aesthetic experience, that is, natural beauty

5 Sociability (friendship)

6 Practical reasonableness

7 Religion

Such goods are identifiable psychologically through 'corresponding inclinations and urges of one's nature'.

The values or goods need no rationale to justify or explain them, and for Finnis are all equally fundamental and 'equally self-evidently a form of good'. In addition, one cannot 'be analytically reduced to being merely an aspect of any of the others'.

Principles of practical reasonableness

As well as Finnis' proposals for basic values, he suggests nine principles of practical reasonableness which assist an individual in life with the aim of fulfilling the 'basic forms of good'. The nine principles are as follows:

1 To do good and avoid evil.

2 To have a rational and coherent life plan.

3 To not arbitrarily prioritise one basic good over another.

4 To treat everyone as equal.

5 To remain objective but not let detachment lead to indifferences, and to maintain commitment to the ideals of the basic goods and be efficient in our moral actions.

6 To limit the relevance of consequences.

> **Key quote**
>
> 'Natural law theory accepts that law can be considered and spoken of both as a sheer social fact of power and practice and as a set of reasons for action that can be and often are sound as reasons and therefore normative for reasonable people addressed by them.'
>
> (John Finnis)

> **Key quote**
>
> 'In voluntarily acting from human goods and avoiding what is opposed to them, one ought to choose and will only those possibilities whose willing is compatible with integral human fulfilment.'
>
> (John Finnis' first moral principle)

> **Key quotes**
>
> 'It is so wonderful to be a rational animal, there is a reason for everything that one does ...'
>
> (John Finnis)
>
> 'One should favor the Common Good by fostering conditions which enable collective Eudaimonia.'
>
> (John Finnis)

> **Exam tip**
>
> To help you remember all the different lists, try to use flashcards and use a practical example for each one – you could even draw an image of the example to help you remember and associate it with a certain teaching.

7 To have respect for every basic value in every act (Finnis holds that in every act one must respect all basic goods).

8 To uphold the requirements of the common good.

9 To follow one's conscience.

Now test yourself   Tested ☐

11 How did Finnis develop Aquinas' theory?

12 List three of the principles of practical reasonableness.

Answers online

Application to an ethical issue

Approach   Revised ☐

When applying the Natural Law ethical system to ethical issues it is important to identify the key ideas behind this theory; for example, the relevant primary precepts or using Finnis' core basic values. However, it is also important to bear in mind how these are applied and to consider the doctrine of double effect, focusing on intentions, in order to escape error in complex situations or cases.

Abortion   Revised ☐

Application of primary precepts

Those who accept Aquinas' doctrine of Natural Law, and seek to apply this to the issue of abortion, believe that the key primary precept involved here is that of preserving innocent life. Hence the act of abortion is seen as inherently evil because of the intentional and direct killing of an innocent human being. This would apply to all situations including those involving rape or incest.

The debate will then focus on when a **fetus** can be considered as a person. Opinions vary between regarding it as the moment of conception or choosing the time of the appearance of a certain feature, such as neural activity.

The doctrine of double effect

The doctrine of double effect, however, does permit the death of the fetus, but only as a by-product of another act. This means that the intention was not to kill the fetus. For instance, the use of chemotherapy or the performance of a hysterectomy to remove a cancerous uterus, would lead to the death of the fetus. However, as that is not the intention of the act, but rather a by-product, the removal of the cancerous uterus is acceptable.

If there is any other reasonable medical treatment available to save the life of the mother which would not entail harm or death of the fetus, then that action must be chosen instead.

Exam tip

When explaining ethical concepts, try to use an example for each concept you explain. This is really important in practical ethics where the theory is shown to work in practice.

Fetus – the unborn baby from the end of the eighth week after conception (when the major structures have formed) until birth.

Now test yourself

13 What two features of Natural Law need to be considered for a moral issue?

14 What, instead of primary precepts, could you use for an answer that applies Natural Law to an ethical issue?

Answers online

Tested ☐

Issues arising

Many issues arise when studying Natural Law. As it is a system that promotes absolute rules, it is in need of careful consideration in terms of its strengths and weaknesses.

The place of cause at the centre of life

Revised

The issue with Natural Law is whether or not the idea of 'cause' is relevant to ethics, is central to life or whether or not it is correctly perceived.

Cause is *not* the centre of life	Cause is central to life
Things do not always have a specific purpose even if they are a cause.	It appears logical and the idea of cause, effect and end purpose do make sense.
Cause must not be confused with correlation or coincidence – sometimes this is the case and an interpretation of events is ambiguous. Aristotle's view of causes is basic and primitive.	It can be seen to work in conjunction with Kant's summum bonum (see Chapter 2.1).
Is there really a final cause for everything or are we just looking for something that is not there?	Human nature does tend to agree that virtue is the desired end for ethics.
The ideas of evolution, **natural selection**, etc., can explain morality without purpose or end.	
Evidence from modern physics suggests there is no need for explanation and also that there are events that arise due to no apparent cause.	

> **Exam tip**
>
> Try to develop different ways of presenting material. For example, contrast two scholars on the same theory (Aquinas and Finnis) or contrast a view (for example Natural Law) with a contrasting theory (for example), Situation Ethics.

> **Natural selection** – a key mechanism of evolution. It is the principle by which each slight variation, if useful, is preserved and the trait passed on to the next generation.

Strengths and weaknesses of Natural Law

Revised

Strengths of Natural Law	Weaknesses of Natural Law
It is based on what it means to be human. To be human means acting in line with our true nature and following our natural inclinations. When the theory is applied, it assumes the special status of human beings.	There seems to be a mistake in reasoning (fallacy) in identifying morality with another concept (i.e. nature). This is sometimes referred to as the 'naturalistic fallacy'.
It is a universal law, and not relative to culture or a religion.	What does it mean to say an action is 'natural'? Does it just mean that it refers to the action that is common to a particular group?
It appeals to common sense.	Is there a common human nature? Surely the fact that cultures have different values challenges the idea of a common nature; for example, Spartan nature was to kill weak or defective children.
Some versions, for example Finnis', do not need God for its authority.	Some would deny there was any such thing as a human nature.
The primary precepts are common to all. Because it is about following natural inclinations, then the application to a moral issue is always the same, wherever you are and whoever you are.	Darwinism sees natural selection as the source of human nature rather than any divine or rational source and guidance. This damages the justification and authority of Natural Law theory.
It gives a clear basis for morality. There is an authority and a clear justification.	If there is a constant unchanging human nature and a natural law that stems from it, how is it that so many through the centuries have got human nature so wrong (for example, slavery and apartheid being considered natural)?
It is clear how Natural Law is applied. For instance, the primary precepts are clearly identified and justified. It is clear for all to see why abortion is wrong.	Human nature seems to change. For instance, the debate about homosexuality has raised questions about what is natural.

Strengths of Natural Law	Weaknesses of Natural Law
Its application seems clear. Again, the application of the primary precepts is straightforward. It is clear how to apply them.	The doctrine of double effect assumes that a sharp distinction can be drawn between directly intending a result and merely foreseeing it. If a result can be foreseen, then in performing the action the person must be intending the consequence?
The doctrine of double effect allows for possible conflicts of primary precepts.	It is difficult to see how those who accept the doctrine of fallen humanity, and therefore the moral imperfection of the human mind, can have such faith in human reasoning when applied to moral issues. If Aquinas could have been wrong about primary precepts, he could also have been wrong about secondary precepts.
	Consequentialist systems are preferable because they are more flexible.

Typical mistake

Instead of just listing things for AO2, make sure that they form part of your own analysis and argument.

Is there such a thing as natural good?

Revised

When the world is so varied and there are so many different views about morality, in the light of all this can there be such a thing as an absolute, natural good?

Natural good exists	Natural good does *not* exist
Universal recognition of morality – every sane person recognises good and bad.	It depends too much on opinion and interpretation.
A biological good, e.g. health, is a natural good of the body, the way it should be.	Can 'natural' and 'good' be used together – for example, nature can be perceived to be cruel.
Aquinas' distinction between apparent and real goods explains any inconsistencies.	Universality is questioned – if there is natural good then why cannot everyone see it and agree on it?
It could be argued that the idea of telos for the world and humanity implies natural good.	Some reject a religious perception of natural good as established by a deity.
The idea of natural good being integral to religion, society, etc.	Do we share a common human nature to establish natural good?

Exam tip

Try different ways of evaluating. Begin with a question, contrast arguments one by one, or even attack a particular viewpoint using evidence to support your argument.

Typical mistake

Evaluation can become mechanical and a list of points. You should investigate the material and demonstrate reasoning.

How compatible is Natural Law with a religious approach to ethics?

Revised

Once again, it is important to consider whether or not Natural Law is compatible with religious approaches to ethics, given that there are many religious people who use the ethical system.

Compatible	InCompatible
The idea that God establishes moral laws supports the idea of moral absolutes.	Natural Low is in stark contrast to teleological, consequential systems such as **Situation Ethics** and Utilitarianism, which are also used by religious believers, and therefore such believers would reject the compatibility of Natural Law.
Some Christians would indicate that the Ten Commandments are clear examples of Natural Law at work – examples of secondary precepts of Finnis' basic values or Aquinas' primary precepts.	The inflexibility of an absolutist system is inconsistent with the ideas of forgiveness, tolerance and non-judgement.
It is the basis of Roman Catholic theology.	If a system is therefore inflexible, it can mean that the application of it can appear to be lacking compassion and clearly inconsistent with religious teachings such as 'turn the other cheek' and 'forgiveness'.
Finnis uses it to support Roman Catholic ethics. There are clear parallels with other ethical theories which are religious; for example, Kant, who had a religious approach in his postulates (see Chapter 2.1).	Finnis has shown that a Natural Law system can be totally independent of God as humans make their own decisions and the law is autonomous and independent of religion.
The practice of casuistry is integral to religious ethics as it is a form of Natural Law; for example, it uses primary and secondary precepts like Aquinas did.	
The idea of an ultimate good and conscience is compatible with religious teaching.	

Exam tip

Make sure that you allow enough time for your AO2 answer.

Situation Ethics – a theory of ethics according to which moral rules are not absolutely binding but may be modified in the light of specific situations.

Now test yourself

Tested

15 Make a list of the issues arising and match the following points to the relevant issue:
   (a) Aquinas' distinction between apparent and real goods explains any inconsistencies.
   (b) Finnis has shown that a Natural Law system can be totally independent of God as human beings make their own decisions and the law is autonomous and independent of religion.
   (c) Human nature does tend to agree that virtue is the desired end for ethics.
   (d) Some would deny there was any such thing as a human nature.
   (e) Can 'natural' and 'good' be used together – for example, nature can be perceived to be cruel?
   (f) It is the basis of Roman Catholic theology.
   (g) Its application seems clear. Again, the application of the primary precepts is straightforward. It is clear how to apply them.
   (h) The ideas of evolution, natural selection, etc., can explain without purpose or end.

Answers online

Exam practice

(a) Explain Aquinas' development of the idea of Natural Law. (30 marks)

(b) 'Aquinas' system of Natural Law ethics is outdated.' Assess this claim. (15 marks)

Answers online

Online

2.3 Religious views of the created world

Narratives of the creation of the world by God

Cosmology is the scientific study of the origin and nature of the universe. The universe is more than just our solar system: it includes every physical thing that exists. Theories about the origins of the universe could raise questions about the meaning and value of human life and ultimately link to moral responsibility.

Religion provides an answer to the question of how it all started through creation narratives.

> **Cosmology** – the study of the origin and nature of the universe.

Key quote

'For thousands of years people have looked up at the heavens and found themselves inspired to contemplate the nature of the universe … To wonder about the nature of the universe is one of the most characteristic of human traits.'

(William Kaufman, physicist)

Christianity

Revised

Creationism

Creationism, as it is normally understood, is a belief that the universe and life were created by God over a very short period of time. The view is anti-evolutionary because it suggests a sudden and complete process rather than one that stretches for countless millions of years. It is often associated with a very literal interpretation of religious texts, such as the creation account in Genesis.

> **Creationism** – the idea that God literally made the world in six days.

The Genesis account

The main source for the Christian view of creation of the universe (and life) is the first and second chapters of Genesis. It depicts God as creating the universe (and life) in eight divine acts over a period of six days:

- Let there be light (Genesis 1:3).
- Let there be an expanse [heaven] between the waters … (Genesis 1:6).
- Let the water under the sky be gathered together … (Genesis 1:9).
- Let the land produce vegetation … (Genesis 1:11).
- Let there be lights in the expanse of the sky … (Genesis 1:14).
- Let the water teem with living creatures, and let birds fly … (Genesis 1:20).
- Let the land produce living creatures … (Genesis 1:24).
- Let us make man in our image … (Genesis 1:26).

It is important to note that a substantial majority of those who would call themselves Christians do not take a strictly literal view of the Genesis account of creation and would accept some kind of evolutionary process.

Different understandings of the narrative

Biblical literalists believe that the seven days in the Genesis account correspond exactly to seven 24-hour days of history during which God

Key quote

'In the beginning God created the heavens and the earth.'

(Genesis 1:1)

Key quote

'By the seventh day God had finished the work he had been doing; so on the seventh day he rested from all his work. And God blessed the seventh day and made it holy, because on it he rested from all the work of creating that he had done.'

(Genesis 2:2–3)

created the world. This results in understanding the creation not in terms of billions of years but rather thousands. Such a view is often referred to as Young Earth creationism (see Chapter 4.2).

Various other understandings and interpretations have been given to the Genesis account. Many believe in God as the Creator without taking a strictly literal view of the whole of Genesis 1–2. Some of the various theories of such people are described here, although this list is not exhaustive:

● Progressive creationism or 'day-age theory' holds that each day of creation week represents a long age (millions or even billions of years) in which God acted upon creation. Supporters of this theory see no reason to interpret the days in a literal sense, since God's time is not the same as our time.

● Gap theory argues that a gap should be inserted between Genesis 1:1 and Genesis 1:2, that is, the creation of the 'heavens and the earth' and the creation of light on the first day. This then accommodates geological time.

● The framework interpretation response sees Genesis 1 as written to provide a theology of creation, and is not to be taken as a scientifically or historically accurate record. This is often expressed as: 'Science answers the how question, while religion answers the why question.'

● There is a view that sees God as the source of the Big Bang. This theory says that the universe had a beginning, and that both time and space came from nothing. This is seen as a parallel to the beginning of Genesis. In 1951 Pope Pius XII declared approval for the **Big Bang theory**, based on this understanding.

> **Big Bang theory** – the theory of an expanding universe that began as infinitely dense energy at some finite time in the past; the initial explosion that caused it to expand is called the Big Bang.

Exam tip

Always remember to show that you understand a topic by avoiding lists in your answer; be more selective and explain how the different aspects you have selected are relevant to the answer. This demonstrates that 'information is accurate and relevant' (AO1).

Key quote

'When it comes to actual physical phenomena, science wins hands down against gods and miracles. That is not to say that science can explain everything. There remain some pretty big gaps: for example, scientists don't know how life began.'

(Paul Davies, physicist)

Typical mistake

Sometimes candidates start to explain one thing and then get carried away and move from the focus of the question. Stay focused!

Now test yourself

Tested ☐

1 Explain two different ways in which a religion may understand its creation narrative.

2 Outline four key elements for the creation narrative of the religion you have studied.

Answers online

Themes within the creation narratives

All creation narratives or the explanations for our existence contain within them teachings about the nature of God and in return the nature of human beings and their purpose for being here. You have studied three of these themes.

The views that this world, created by God, must be the best possible world

Revised

Christian

The Christian creation story clearly has within it the message of how 'good' the creation is. This has been taken further by theologians and philosophers to mean that it is therefore the best of all possible worlds.

There are three clear stages of justification for this view:

1 The first involves an understanding of the Hebrew '**tam**' that occurs in Genesis 1 and is translated as 'good'. Its meaning is much debated and it is translated in different ways, often as 'good' or 'perfect' but its best rendering is probably 'mature', 'complete', 'whole' or, as we may say, 'the finished article'. In other words, it is completely fit for purpose.

2 The second stage includes philosophical deliberations over the all-loving nature of God that must reflect perfection and ultimate good. That this is 'the best possible world' might be asserted in connection with the totality of God's attributes, since an all-powerful, all-knowing and perfect creator might be supposed to produce the best possible world.

3 The third stage was best defined by the philosopher Leibniz, who explored the implications of what the best possible world actually was. Since the beginning of Christianity, debates have been held to consider the apparent contradiction of an all-powerful and all-loving God creating a less than perfect world. In essence, Leibniz argued that the best possible world had to be a world wherein the balance of good is greater than evil, hence allowing for what Augustine called the 'fall' of humanity from grace and perfection into sin and imperfection.

However, this calls into question the nature of that which is good, as it inherently contains evil. This then gave rise to the later '**theodicies**' of Christian theologians who defend the nature of God and God's 'fallen' creation in the light of the presence of evil. For example, Richard Swinburne, professor of philosophy, argues that this world is the best one of several possibilities. Some thinkers have also used quantum physics to justify the world as a creation of God, in that it is the optimisation of God's plan through multiple universes.

Key quote

'God saw all that he had made, and it was very good. And there was evening, and there was morning – the sixth day.'

(Genesis 1:31)

Tam – the Hebrew word for 'good', 'perfect', 'whole' or 'complete'.

Theodicy – a justification of the righteousness of God, given the existence of evil.

Exam tip

This section is full of new concepts. In your revision, instead of just drawing up a glossary of key words, try changing this into a flowchart that links each aspect of the topic together. This will help to demonstrate 'good understanding' of the topic overall (AO1).

Now test yourself

3 For the religion(s) that you have studied, outline three reasons why this world is the best possible world.

Answer online

Tested

The world created according to God's intentions

Revised

Christianity

Within Christianity the teaching about creation encompasses the idea of teleology or purpose. The world was made for a purpose and central to this was humanity. This thinking can be found in Natural Law theory, whereby human beings use reason to work out appropriate behaviour. However, it could also extend to God's intentions with regard to an overall ultimate plan. Indeed, the idea of Christ the **redeemer** and the plan of **resurrection** to an afterlife are crucial to this plan.

Redeemer – the idea that something can be brought back or put right.

Resurrection – to come back from the dead.

In terms of ethical theory, it has often been argued that a human being's conscience is a guide for them in matters of ethical concern. For many Christians, this conscience is viewed as an inner voice of God that communicates divine intentions.

Now test yourself

Tested ☐

4   For the religion(s) that you have studied, outline three factors that indicate that the world was made according to God's intentions.

Answer online

God sustains the created world

Revised ☐

Christianity

Unlike the ancient Greek understanding of a 'first cause' that initiates the world but then remains distant and unattached to it, there is within Christianity a very different understanding of the role of God in creation. This can be summarised in the following way:

- God is intricately involved in creation (Genesis 1).
- God sustains the universe according to divine will and in line with its overall purpose. (Professor of philosophy Frederick Copleston extended the ancient Greek idea of 'cause' to argue that God is the efficient cause that controls all other causes in a hierarchy of causes.)
- God establishes and maintains order. (See, for example, Psalms 90–100.)
- God has a relationship with humanity as chosen people and 'sons and daughters'.
- Existence and therefore humanity is dependent upon God. (Paul Tillich, the theologian, famously referred to God as the '**ground of being**'.)
- God communicates with humanity through the Holy Spirit.
- God intervenes in the world, as is seen in biblical history.

Despite all this, it is Christian understanding that God still remains distinct from the universe and is **transcendent**.

Ground of being – the idea that existence is dependent upon God, put forward by theologian Paul Tillich.

Transcendent – wholly independent of (and removed from) the material universe.

Exam tip

When answering a question on God sustaining the world, make sure that you focus on the area highlighted in the question. Make sure you pick out the key points and explain why they are important in relation to the question. This ensures that you focus on the question and that 'information is mostly accurate and relevant' (AO1).

Now test yourself

Tested ☐

5   For the religion(s) that you have studied, outline three ways in which the world is sustained by God or universal principles.

Answer online

The status and duty of humankind in the created world

Status in the created world

In Christianity, humanity has a special status as humans are reflections of God. According to some Christian thinkers, their purpose is to develop and grow into the 'likeness' of God as they progress through life.

Duty in the created world

According to the first Genesis story of creation, the environment and all creatures in it were made before humanity and it is part of human responsibility as stewards to look after and care for the world. Genesis 1:27–28 talks about humans 'ruling over' the world and the animals. What this actually means has led to some debate. Many Christians accept that human beings were given a responsibility from God to look after and care for both the environment and animals, and therefore humans beings are seen as more important. This is often referred to as **stewardship**.

The status of the non-human world

Teachings from the different religions about care for the environment may be relevant and can be found in Chapter 2.4. This section concerns itself mainly with animals.

> **Key quote**
>
> 'Then God said, "Let us make man in our image, in our likeness, and let them rule over the fish of the sea and the birds of the air, over the livestock over all the earth, and over all the creatures that move along the ground." So God created man in his own image, in the image of God he created him; male and female he created them.'
>
> (Genesis 1:26–27)

> **Stewardship** – a duty to look after and care for something on behalf of somebody else.

Christianity and animals

The Genesis story clearly states that God created the world and it was 'good'. Human beings are nevertheless still the most important of creation, but this does not mean that the rest of creation is worthless. On the contrary, other creatures are witness to the glory of God, although the traditional Christian teaching is that they do not have souls nor the capacity to reason. Some modern Christian thinking gives a greater value to animals, pointing out that God made a covenant with them as well and that the Garden of Eden, as a picture of the ideal world, gives them peace and security as much as humanity.

The understanding of the word 'ruling' or '**dominion**' has led to different interpretations of the role of human beings towards animals. Some Christians believe that animals do not have the same rights as humans but their teaching focuses on the duties that human beings have towards animals. They believe animals should be looked after and cared for properly but that animals are not level with human beings. They therefore would always put human rights above those of animals. In contrast, Quakers believe that that they should show consideration for all of God's creatures and one aspect of this could be to stand up for the rights of animals. They would try to balance the rights of human beings with kindness towards animals and attempt to bring about the good of both.

> **Dominion** – in Christianity, a word meaning responsibility for the created world.

> **Exam tip**
>
> Always point out the variety of religious ideas in an answer. This enables a demonstration of 'good understanding ... through use of evidence and examples' (AO1 descriptor) and also builds up and will help any following 'analysis' (AO2 descriptor).

> **Typical mistake**
>
> It is good to prepare and practise answers; however, do not simply repeat a prepared answer but instead use the information in it to answer the question that is set on the paper. Always stay focused on the question asked.

Some Christians may feel that they were given the role by God to look after and care for animals and so become vegetarians. On the other hand, while a Christian could not possibly advocate torture or cruelty, they would perhaps use this to justify domesticating animals, zoos, and the meat industry. Indeed, it was God who first slaughtered animals 'The Lord God made garments of skin for Adam and his wife and clothed them'. (Genesis 3:21). It was also God who demanded sacrifice throughout the Old Testament, for example a lamb instead of Isaac (Genesis 22:8). Testing on animals for medical reasons could be argued to be the lesser of two evils, as animals do not have a soul.

Issues arising

Now test yourself

6　For the religion(s) that you have studied, describe a key teaching about the status of humanity.

7　For the religion(s) that you have studied, outline two duties of humanity.

8　For the religion(s) that you have studied, outline three teachings about animals.

Answers online

Tested

Is God's world perfect and must it be so?　　　Revised

There is a debate that springs from the idea that God's world is perfect that actually looks at the world and argues that it may not be perfect. This then leads to the question of whether or not an imperfect world can be reconciled with the idea of a perfect God. There are a number of arguments in support of and against this.

In support	Against
The Hebrew word 'tam' has been interpreted by many to mean 'perfect'.	There are different understandings of the Hebrew word 'tam' that suggest that it is not meant as 'perfect' but is better translated as 'complete' or 'whole', which is very different.
God's attributes are traditionally ones of perfection and so anything that is the product of God must also be perfect.	A major objection to the idea of perfection is the existence of free will, and also that the idea of **redemption** of humanity through the death and resurrection of Jesus is in God's overall plan.
The theory of Natural Law is one that confirms that the world has a set law and order to which it works and that it is our role as human beings to tease this out through reason.	The problem of evil and suffering that exists in the world demonstrates that the world is not perfect.
The definition of the word 'perfection' for some people actually means 'perfect for purpose' in that it does the job it needs to do.	The central teachings that human beings are sinful creatures (the Fall) indicate that the world is not perfect.
The theodicy (defences of God in the face of evil and suffering) of Augustine exonerates God of all responsibility for any imperfections that arise.	Irenaeus (ce130–202) argued that God actually allows for the use of evil to achieve a state of perfection.

Redemption – to be brought back. In Christian terms, to be delivered from sin.

Exam tip

For an AO2 answer, include some key questions and make sure that you offer more than one possible conclusion and then give your own, reasoned opinion based upon what you have chosen to write about. This ensures that 'there is some critical analysis' (AO2).

Typical mistake

Do not just write about one viewpoint in your evaluation.

Now test yourself

Tested

Answers online

9 For the religion(s) that you have studied, list two arguments why the/God's world must be perfect.

10 For the religion(s) that you have studied, give two reasons why the world may not have to be perfect.

The ethical implications of the idea that God sustains creation

Revised

If God has a role in creation – that is, if God is involved directly with humanity – then this raises ethical issues for religious believers concerning the nature of both humanity and God.

In support of an ethical world	Against an ethical world
There is a clear guide for moral order if God is sustaining creation.	A God that allows evils such as the Holocaust cannot be ethical.
God will ensure that the world maintains and fulfils its purpose.	There is clearly evil and suffering and so God cannot be all loving.
God is a God of justice and needs to sustain justice throughout the world.	If God chooses to sustain the world then why, when God intervenes in the world, does God choose some and not others? This is clearly unethical.
God has to sustain the world by allowing evil in order for the greater good to be achieved, but this needs to be carefully balanced and nurtured.	If God sustains the world, then the managing of this is very erratic.
Free will.	There is strong case to argue that creation is slowly being destroyed and not sustained.

Now test yourself

Tested

11 For the religion(s) that you have studied, list two ethical problems associated with God intervening in the world.

Answer online

Exam tip

Be careful when using quotes to critically analyse. Always make sure that the quote relates to the argument that is presented. To make sure of this, explain the relevance of the quote in your answer. This ensures that 'different views are clearly explained with supporting evidence and argument' (AO2).

Religious views about the status and duty of humans and non-humans in the created world

Revised

Religions present a detailed picture of how human beings interact with the planet in accordance with the wishes of the divine or universal principles of life (Buddhism). However, how valid are such understandings?

Strengths

- There is a clear role given, such as stewardship.
- Human beings have a responsibility for the world through their relationship with God.
- The idea of creation for humanity implies a personal involvement and duty of care.
- Religious teachings about moral behaviour are characterised by compassion.
- Animals are treated with care according to stewardship in Christianity.

Typical mistake

Try to make sure that your points are not just lists of arguments that do not link together.

Weaknesses

- Human beings are ignorant or have a sinful nature and so are not capable of following their duty.
- The view of the created world in religion is anthropomorphic in focus and the resulting status of humanity leads to biased views about the importance and significance of the non-human world.
- Gaia theory (see Chapter 2.4) suggests there is a much more holistic model to the world and argues that it is a self-sustaining and regulating phenomenon.
- There is a lack of consistency in religious teachings.
- There is evidence of exploitation of animals throughout history.
- Human beings continue with animal experimentation.
- Animals do not have souls according to Christian teaching.

Exam tip

Always make sure that you draw a conclusion from the arguments that you have put forward. This does not necessarily have to agree with an argument. Your conclusion may be that questions are unanswered. You may even want to finish with your own 'further questions' in response to the debate. This means that an 'appropriate evaluation is supported by reasoned argument' (AO2).

Now test yourself

Tested

12 For the religion(s) that you have studied, outline two strengths of the views about human status and duty.
13 For the religion(s) that you have studied, outline two weaknesses of the views about human status and duty.
14 For the religion(s) that you have studied, outline two strengths of the views about non-human status and duty.
15 For the religion(s) that you have studied, outline two weaknesses of the views about non-human status and duty.

Answers online

Exam practice

(a) Explain what is meant by the view that any world created by God must be the best of all possible worlds. (30 marks)

(b) 'The view that this world is perfect is totally inaccurate.' Discuss how far this is true. (15 marks)

Answers online

Online

2.4 Environment, both local and worldwide

Threats to the environment

The discipline of **environmental ethics** has several concerns:

- To measure the impact that human beings have on our planet biologically in terms of pollution and damage to ecosystems, and how human beings, affect both other living beings and vegetation.

- To measure the impact that human beings have on geology and climate.

- To measure the impact that human beings have on our planet aesthetically.

- To consider long-term and short-term solutions to major problems posed by human impact.

- To challenge all threats to the environment.

- To educate people concerning the impact that human beings have on all areas of the environment.

> **Environmental ethics** – the discipline of studying the impact of human action on the environment and deciding what is the correct course of action to take.

Pollution and its consequences
`Revised ☐`

Pollution is one major environmental concern. As a species, human beings cause pollution to our planet in several ways:

- Litter
- Non-recyclable waste materials
- Toxic and nuclear waste
- Oil spillages affecting seas and rivers
- Sewage
- Industrial waste and carbon emissions
- Increased use of '**greenhouse gases**'

> **Greenhouse gases** – those gases that impact upon the planet so as to increase global temperatures like a 'greenhouse effect'.

Global warming and pollution

One of the major threats of pollution is global warming. Global warming impacts upon sea levels, climate change (including the increased severity of storms and changing weather patterns), and an overall shift and change in the infrastructure of our planet. It melts ice caps, affecting the biodiversity of an ecosystem by threatening the wildlife, and poses potential extinction of species. Sea levels impact on the availability of habitable land. There are also other threats to the environment caused by pollution:

- Chemicals in the atmosphere cause acid rain, which has long been a major concern and threatens trees.

- Advances in industry, science and technology for commercial gain do not consider the long-term impact.

- Pollution impacts indirectly on agriculture, causing crop failure or even crop pollution.

- Landfills for waste and safe disposal areas for toxic waste are becoming increasingly hard to find and both pose a potential threat to animals and human safety.
- There is an impact on developing nations, many of which are rapidly destroying their environment through industry (see below).
- **Deforestation** has adverse affects on the land and on the global climate.
- The use of finite non-renewable energy resources and the burning of fossil fuels also have adverse consequences.
- The poor will suffer more than the rich (see below).

These are just a few of the problems raised and, just as with any society, it is a duty for humanity on a global scale to be responsible for our actions. This means our actions towards the environment.

> **Deforestation** – the cutting down of trees for commercial use of the land.

> **Exam tip**
>
> Always point out the *variety* of religious ideas in an answer. This enables a demonstration of 'good understanding ... through use of evidence and examples' (AO1 descriptor) and also builds up and will help any following 'analysis' (AO2 descriptor).

Now test yourself   Tested ☐

1 What does environmental ethics concern itself with?
2 List three examples of pollution.
3 Explain three examples of the consequences of pollution.

Answers online

> **Typical mistake**
>
> Make sure that you time your answers carefully and correctly for AO1 answers and that you have enough time left to answer the (AO2) section.

The living and non-living environment   Revised ☐

Some countries have long had laws concerning matters such as waste disposal because of the immediate impact it has. Many now call for new laws and international agreements to tackle other more devastating actions globally that threaten our planet in the longer term.

One recent example of this global approach is concern over 'carbon footprints'. Even supermarkets are now measuring the impact of their products on the environment for consumers to see and consequently influence them to spend responsibly on sustainable goods. This is one small way of responding.

From a religious perspective, the idea of a creator God implies an idyllic world with humanity as having a key role to play in its care: In Christianity, human beings were given '**dominion**' and Adam was told to 'till the soil'.

> **Dominion** – in Christianity, a word meaning responsibility for the created world.

In terms of the living environment, movements such as the WWF (the World Wildlife Fund) and individuals such as the philosopher Peter Singer have long protested the rights of animals and feel that we have a duty of care and respect for fellow beings on the planet. Anyone who acknowledges the superiority of the human race over other species, according to Singer, is no better than a racist (*Animal Liberation*, 1995). The message is clear. We are all in this together.

Recent actions by governments   Revised ☐

In recent years there has been a recognition by governments of the need to act on a global scale. One significant response was the **Kyoto Protocol** (1997), which aims to combat global warming by creating an international treaty on the environment with the targets of 'stabilisation of greenhouse gas concentrations in the atmosphere at a level that would prevent

> **Kyoto Protocol** – a code of behaviour for everyone to follow in reducing emissions globally.

dangerous anthropogenic interference with the climate system'. Although 191 countries have signed the treaty, the USA has not.

Another example of the recognition to act is the tradition of **Earth Summits**. The most recent was Rio in 2012, which aimed to promote sustainable development but also unite economic and environmental policies of the global community. At the end of the summit, over 190 nations agreed to a plan for global sustainable development by strengthening global environmental management, tightening protection of the oceans, improving food security and promoting a 'green economy'. Members of the summit were positive, although there have been criticisms of it being 'all talk and no real action' and accusations have been made that the decisions made are driven by underlying commercial aims.

The criticism is mainly that environmental concerns are not a priority and until they are, meaningful progress cannot be achieved.

We can see that the consequences of acts of pollution over a long period of time have a devastating impact on the environment, sometimes directly and sometimes indirectly. Sometimes the problem is that people do not understand the complexity of an ecosystem in that one action can have an impact on several areas, and in several directions, just like the release of a line of dominoes that are toppled. In addition, as highlighted above, there is not just the impact(s) of one action to consider but the impacts of many.

However, in the same way, a positive action is one that can have a dramatic impact in the reverse direction and so too impact on several areas. Thus the Kyoto Protocol and the Earth Summits are potentially powerful.

The message from all quarters is that we have an obligation to look after the planet because it is worth saving for our future and for future generations. It is vital to act, and despite all criticisms, it is important to play a role individually and not adopt a defeatist attitude.

There is a well-known story of an old man who daily spends his time on a beach throwing back the starfish into the ocean to save them. Despite his efforts, many are still washed ashore. An onlooker after a few days asks the man why he bothers when ultimately it makes no difference. The old man picks up a starfish, throws it back into the ocean and turns to face the onlooker saying, 'Well it made a difference to that one.'

> **Earth Summits** – meetings of nations to discuss and act on environmental concerns.

> **Key quote**
>
> 'We didn't get the Future We Want in Rio, because we do not have the leaders we need. The leaders of the most powerful countries supported business as usual, shamefully putting private profit before people and the planet.'
>
> (Greenpeace International Executive Director, Kumi Naidoo, quoted in the *Guardian*, 23 June 2012)

> **Key quote**
>
> 'Since the first summit in 1992, global emissions have risen by 48 per cent, 300 million hectares of forest have been cleared and the population has increased by 1.6 billion people. Despite a reduction in poverty, one in six people are malnourished.'
>
> (*Guardian*, 23 June 2012)

Protection of the environment

Revised

There are many ways in which humanity can protect the environment from further harm – both the living creatures in it and the non-living world. Here are some ways in which humans can and do strive to protect the environment:

- Recycle materials at all levels from individual to industry, from local to national and international.
- Look for more aesthetic and efficient ways of disposing of waste.
- Protect areas of outstanding natural beauty, **greenbelt** land, etc.

> **Greenbelt** – an area of protected countryside.

- Re-evaluate agricultural methods.
- Limit the use of fossil fuels.
- Explore alternative ways of generating electricity, e.g. solar power is becoming more popular.
- Adhere to international agreements as outlined by the 2012 Earth Summit and meet the figures agreed by the Kyoto Protocol.
- Make sure toxic waste is securely and safely disposed of with minimum impact on the environment.
- Make sure that indirect determining factors are addressed to eradicate the root of environmental problems, e.g. sustainable development in the developing world, sanctions against dictators, war against poverty, limiting devastation through conflict.
- Provide medical support to control the spread of disease, etc.
- Take a more species-friendly approach to animal testing, recognising the rights of other species.
- Become actively involved in situations where a species is threatened by extinction, e.g. mountain gorillas threatened by loss of habitat, war and poaching due to poverty and illegal trade.

Preservation of the environment ———————————————— Revised ☐

Preservation of the environment concerns itself with longer-term, sustainable ways of improving conditions and slowly redressing the current imbalance. Conservation efforts could include some of the following:

- Government backing, sponsorship and support of renewable energy resources.
- Raising awareness through education.
- Conservation agendas for forests, wetlands, greenbelt areas, national parks (including animal parks), forests, sea and lake areas.
- Preventing further destruction of forests, etc., and replanting devastated areas.
- Anti-pollution campaigns and designating some areas as pollution free.
- Limiting traffic congestion with tolls that feed back into conservation funds.
- Gradual changeover to more environmentally-friendly fuel systems.
- The work of environmental agencies, e.g. Friends of the Earth, Greenpeace, WWF.

James Lovelock's Gaia theory ———————————————— Revised ☐

An interesting take on the world as we know it is James Lovelock's **Gaia theory**. The name Gaia was suggested by the author and close friend of James Lovelock, William Golding, after the Greek goddess of the Earth.

In the 1960s James Lovelock proposed that the Earth was in a condition of full homeostasis. That is, the Earth's biomass alters certain conditions to make it a more hospitable environment and also functions as a single organism that maintains conditions necessary for its survival.

> **Gaia theory** – James Lovelock's theory that the Earth regulates and sustains itself over time in order to survive.

In other words, our environment is inextricably connected because it is an organic whole and, just like our human bodies, responds to exterior changes in order to survive or heal itself. It was seen as a way to explain the fact that combinations of chemicals including oxygen and methane persist in stable concentrations in the atmosphere of the Earth.

James Lovelock defined Gaia as:

> a complex entity involving the Earth's biosphere, atmosphere, oceans, and soil; the totality constituting a feedback or cybernetic system which seeks an optimal physical and chemical environment for life on this planet.

Some have interpreted this to mean that the Earth is a single organism that regulates and maintains itself. However, it is clear that this is not seen to be driven by a conscious self-awareness of the holistic picture but rather as a more 'Darwinian' quest for survival.

It is important to note that Gaia theory challenges the idea of 'dominion' or humanity's control of the world. It could be that in the grand scheme of things, we, as a human species, become less significant than the dinosaurs.

Until 1975 the hypothesis was almost totally ignored. An article in the *New Scientist* of 15 February 1975 began to attract scientific and critical attention to the hypothesis. In 1979 the book *Gaia: A New Look at Life on Earth* was published.

Now test yourself

Tested ☐

4 What are 'Earth Summits'?
5 List three ways to protect the environment.
6 List three ways to preserve the environment.

Answers online

Key quote

'The Gaia theory posits that the organic and inorganic components of Planet Earth have evolved together as a single living, self-regulating system. It suggests that this living system has automatically controlled global temperature, atmospheric content, ocean salinity, and other factors, that maintains its own habitability.'

(Taken from www.gaiatheory.org)

Exam tip

Do not answer a question by simply 'giving a descriptive account'. Your answer should always select the key events, that is, the appropriate information relevant to the question. This demonstrates more personal understanding or 'ownership' of the knowledge. It is evidence that 'information is mostly accurate and relevant' (AO1).

Typical mistake

Sometimes candidates start to explain one thing and then get carried away and move from the focus of the question. Stay focused!

The Third World

Revised ☐

There are many problems and potential problems with the emerging economies classed within the '**Third World**'. As well as the North–South divide (where the richest 25 per cent of the world uses 80 per cent of the resources, leaving 75 per cent to share 20 per cent of the world's resources), there are growing economies within the South with enormous internal inequalities. One example is India which, as well as having mass poverty, also has one of the most influential economies in the world, growing (and polluting) at an exponential rate.

Some may argue that it appears morally hypocritical for the developed world to approach the Third World and ask the countries to stop polluting. There are already countless problems in the developing world such as wars, debt, lack of education, disease, low life expectancy and a lack of clean fresh water, all of which contribute to the melting pot of environmental damage either directly or indirectly. In addition, there are many corrupt, self-appointed governments whose priority appears to be commercial rather than environmental. However, the often unrestrained growth of industries burning fossil fuels and the unchecked deforestation and devastation of lands for cash crops are having a detrimental effect

Third World – general description for developing countries (though other terms may be preferable).

upon the environment. Even though much damage has already been caused, the sheer volume of geographical space and population taken up by the developing world makes the potential for environmental catastrophe more real.

Ethical issues and the developing Third World

There are several ethical issues associated with the emergence of the developing countries:

- The developed world not allowing the developing world the same advantages it had in becoming wealthy and powerful.
- The restriction of people from the developing world from bettering themselves.
- The hypocrisy in that much of the industry in the Third World that causes environmental damage is actually owned by investors from the developed world who are unwilling to invest ethically because it is not so profitable.
- Heavy dependence on fossil fuels contributes to global warming.
- There are no strict safety procedures or controls on the waste of industrial development, leading to further pollution and a knock-on effect of poor health, poverty and starvation.
- Factory developments are taking place in areas of natural beauty.
- Countries involved in conflicts and feuds are more concerned with developing military power than saving the environment.
- The developed world is not willing to pay for restricting the developing world's development and compensate for loss in quality of life.
- Nor is the developed world willing to invest in restricting growth and development – the USA and China still cannot agree on their own reduction of emissions let alone control another's!

Attempts to restrict development

- A call to restrict fuel emissions despite the lack of ability to generate electricity via nuclear reactors.
- Oil-producing countries have no incentive to stop producing oil rather than investing in alternative sources of energy.
- The main attempts to restrict the development of the Third World in terms of environmental damage are directly related to the extent to which the by-products of expanding an industrial base can be controlled. For example, can we restrict pollution?
  - Can rivers and lakes be free of industrial effluent?
  - Can factory development be restricted as in the developed world to protect the environment in certain areas?
  - Can areas of outstanding natural beauty and animal conservation areas be protected?
  - Can population pressure that causes further problems be alleviated?
  - Will the developed world be willing not to take advantage of cheap labour and products in order to save the environment?

It is clear that there are a number of questions raised if humanity is to restrict Third World development and reduce the impact of environmental damage.

One solution is to prioritise, just as with the treaties that originated in the developed world to calm environmental impact, and decide which specific issues are the most important such as, for example, preservation of forests, wetlands, wildernesses, areas of natural outstanding beauty and of other species that are endangered.

Nonetheless, it should always be considered that despite whatever call for restraints are presented, many people still feel that humanitarian welfare and the increase in quality of life outweigh environmental needs. It is here that education and awareness-raising are vital.

Now test yourself   Tested ☐

7   What is the North–South divide?
8   State three ethical issues associated with the developing world.
9   State three ways in which the developing world may need to be restricted in its development.

Answers online

Exam tip

Remember to explain each point that you make in an exam answer to the full. Think carefully about each sentence and how it relates to the question and the previous sentence. Aim for at least three sentences to explain a point. For example, state what the point is, how it is understood and then give an example. This will help to ensure 'a thorough treatment of the topic within the time available' (AO1).

Typical mistake

Make sure that in an exam you use your technical information correctly. Do not confuse key terms.

Religious teachings about human responsibility

When looking at specific religious responses, it is also important to know that groups such as Target Earth, Deep Ecology and Greenpeace do have the support of many religious believers who share common aims.

Christianity ———————————————————————— Revised ☐

Christians believe that God made the world (creator) for human beings to 'rule over'. According to the first Genesis story of creation, the environment and all creatures in it were made before humanity and it is part of human responsibility as **stewards** to look after and care for the world. Genesis 1: 27–28 talks about humans 'ruling over' the world and the animals. What this actually means has led to some debate. Many Christians accept that human beings were given a responsibility from God to look after and care for both the environment and animals and therefore humans are seen as more important. This is often referred to as 'stewardship'. For many Christians their responsibility for the planet means they think they should take action to preserve the environment and not do more damage to it. Christians believe that part of this responsibility is to make others aware of the situation and encourage everyone to try and help. Most Christians accept this role, especially as it is mostly because of human activities that the damage has occurred in the first place. They take their responsibility seriously and believe that they must act now in order to help reverse the damage done. An example of this would be the group Target Earth, which buys up threatened land, for example 8000

Steward – someone who is responsible for looking after something.

acres in Belize, to save vegetation (e.g. mahogany trees) and animals (e.g. the jaguar). It also works with local conservation groups in areas where plants and wildlife are threatened and works to restore areas where land has been devastated by human activity such as quarrying. The Assisi Declarations also back this up by teaching that all Christian Churches should be brought together to talk about what science and technology are hoping to achieve and what they are doing to the planet at present. They state that a moral obligation to look after our planet is more important than scientific and technological advances.

Christians and animals

The understanding of the word 'ruling' or 'dominion' has led to different interpretations of the role of humans towards animals. Some Christians believe that animals do not have the same rights as humans but their teaching focuses on the duties that human beings have towards animals. They believe animals should be looked after and cared for properly but that animals are not level with human beings. They therefore would always put human rights above those of animals. In contrast, Quakers believe that that they should show consideration for all of God's creatures and one aspect of this could be to stand up for the rights of animals. They would try to balance the rights of human beings with kindness towards animals and attempt to bring about the good of both. Some Christians may feel that they were given the role by God to look after and care for animals and so become vegetarians. On the other hand while Christians could not possibly advocate torture or cruelty, they would perhaps use this to justify domesticating animals, zoos, and the meat industry. Indeed, it was God who first slaughtered animals (Genesis 3:21) 'The Lord God made garments of skin for Adam and for his wife and clothed them'. It was also God who demanded sacrifice throughout the Old Testament, for example a lamb instead of Isaac (Genesis 22:8). It could be argued to be the lesser of two evils to test on animals for medical reasons as animals do not have a soul.

> **Exam tip**
>
> This section is full of new concepts. In your revision, instead of just drawing up a glossary of key words, try changing this into a flowchart that links each aspect of the topic together. This will help to demonstrate 'good understanding' of the topic overall (AO1).

> **Typical mistake**
>
> It is good to prepare and practise answers; however, do not simply repeat a prepared answer but instead use the information in it to answer the question that is set on the paper. Always stay focused on the question asked.

> **Now test yourself**
>
> 10 Give three reasons why a Christian should look after the environment.
>
> 11 State three teachings from Christianity about animals.
>
> **Answers online**
>
> Tested ☐

Issues arising

Is protection of the environment an issue only for the rich?

Revised ☐

In terms of wealth in the world, there is a clear North–South divide. If you are living in the northern world you are generally in one of the MEDCs (more economically developed countries) – advanced countries that have high standards of living. If you are in the southern world you are generally in one of the LEDCs (less economically developed countries) – these are developing countries with a lower standard of living. As we have seen, 25 per cent of the world's population live in MEDCs, but use 80 per cent of the world's resources; and 75 per cent of the world's population live in LEDCs, but use only 20 per cent of the world's resources.

In support	Against
The rich have more responsibility, having more wealth and influence.	Everyone shares the Earth not just the rich.
Rich countries can solve many of the problems due to their involvement with developing areas.	Future generations need care and this includes rich people and poor people.
Poor people cannot escape their own personal situation, let alone influence worldwide matters of environmental importance.	Anyone can recycle and 'do their bit'.
The rich are the ones who fund the charities that work on environmental issues.	It can all be relative – the rich individuals and countries may want to do more but it can be done as a team effort.
	Most initiatives involve a partnership, e.g. treaties, economic change, international cooperation.
	Just because most charities working for the environment are funded by the wealthy does not mean this is the only way people can change things.

Exam tip

For an AO2 answer, always include some key questions and make sure that you offer more than one possible conclusion; then give your own, reasoned opinion based upon what you have chosen to write about. This ensures that 'there is some critical analysis' (AO2).

Typical mistake

Candidates can often make the mistake of simply repeating one line of argument or perspective in an evaluation. Always make sure that you consider different views in your evaluation.

Is protection of the environment only for the good and benefit of humankind?

Revised

In support	Against
There is a clear case for this in the context of the Genesis story, one reading of which interprets 'dominion' in a way that is in the interests of human beings.	Just because human beings control the protective measures in place does not necessarily mean that protection is for their own sake and not for other species, for example.
In the long term, that protection is to benefit humanity is beyond question as it will be for the benefit of future generations.	The protective measures of wildlife parks and National Parks and the work of WWF benefit animals.
In practical terms, the realities of population increase and needs of human beings may override and dictate the protective measures introduced, so in this way it is the benefit of humankind that dictates the extent to which the environment is protected.	Saving the environment from abuse also benefits the environment itself and not just humanity.
Human beings inevitably wish to avoid the possibility of future extinction as a species.	'Dominion' does not mean self-interest and so Christians see the idea of stewardship as protection for all God's creation.
	The environment is worth saving because it is of value in itself.

Exam tip

In preparing for a question and answer that involves AO2, critical analysis, try to divide your answer into sections that reflect different views. Always use a plan to do this *but* keep it very brief. This helps you in memorising but also in categorising the material in your analysis. The sections can broadly correspond to arguments for, arguments against and arriving at a conclusion. This demonstrates that you have considered 'different views' (AO2).

Typical mistake

Try to make sure that your points are not just lists of arguments that do not link together.

How far should humans be forced to be environmentally responsible?

Revised

In favour of enforcement	Against enforcement
In religion the duty of care (stewardship) may be seen to be an imperative and therefore obligatory not optional.	Human beings have choices and a very basic human right is free will.
People can be indifferent and ignorant and so any awareness-raising should aim to initiate a compulsion to act for the benefit of the environment.	Some religions may argue that human beings have the authority to control the environment and it should not be the other way around.
The environment is our life or death and so we should be compelled as a duty to care for it in order for us to survive.	What a person does on their own land and in their own home is their own business.
Environmental responsibility covers a range of areas and we are already compelled to follow laws that restrict damage, for example litter, waste disposal, protection of greenbelt areas.	It depends on the extent to which one is made to be environmentally responsible.
New laws and agreements show that human beings are willing to be forced to be environmentally responsible in recognising it is the discipline they need to save the environment.	It depends on how serious the consequences would be if we were not forced to be environmentally responsible.
It is in the interest of humanity to be forced to be environmentally responsible and so therefore Utilitarian principles dictate it should be so.	If someone is forced to do something it does not educate them, reform them or make them any the wiser as to the value of the environment.

Exam tip

Be careful when using quotes to analyse critically. Always make sure that a quote relates to the argument that is presented. To make sure of this, explain the relevance of the quote in your answer. This ensures that 'different views' are clearly explained with supporting evidence and argument' (AO2).

Examiner's tip

Make sure that you draw a conclusion from the arguments that you have put forward. This does not necessarily have to agree with an argument. Your conclusion may be that questions are unanswered. You may even want to finish with your own 'further questions' in response to the debate! This means that an 'appropriate evaluation is supported by reasoned argument' (AO2).

Strengths and weaknesses of religious teachings about human responsibility for the environment

Revised

Strengths	Weaknesses
The approach of Christianity promotes tolerance and kindness, promoting stewardship.	An human-centered approach to the environment is not an advantage but only taints any chance of an objective perspective.
The approach of Christianity is holistic in that God created everything and said it was 'good'.	Religious teachings such as Christian values in regards to animals are not always respectful, e.g. humans have souls but animals do not.
The approach of Christianity is androcentric and some see this as a strength.	Religious teachings only suggest perspectives and attitudes and do not insist on action.
The approach of Christianity recognises the environment as God's creation and that it is therefore of great value and importance.	Human beings have reason and so can choose their response, e.g. philosophy or Deep Ecology.
Many religious teachings support the aims of environmental groups.	Religious teachings are of value but other views need to be considered.

Exam practice

(a) Explain how religion helps a religious believer understand the role of humanity with regard to the environment. **(30 marks)**

(b) 'Religious teachings are irrelevant and not effective enough to combat threats to the environment today.' Assess this claim. **(15 marks)**

Answers online

Online

3.1 The cosmological argument

The thrust of the cosmological argument is based on the observation that the universe cannot account for its own existence, and so there must be causes that have their origin in the existence of God. The key question that arises is why something exists rather than nothing. There are various forms of the argument but Aquinas' argument is the one that is required for study for the exam.

Aquinas' argument

The philosopher and theologian Thomas Aquinas (1225–74) wrote a compact form of the arguments for the existence of God and these have become known as the Five Ways. It is the first three ways that deal with the cosmological argument.

The form of the argument

Revised ☐

The First Way: the unmoved mover

This focuses on the idea of change or **motion**:

1 An object has the potential to become something different, so movement (or change) is the fulfilment of that potential.

2 Nothing can be both potential and actual at the same time. When something is potential it hasn't happened and so cannot be actual.

3 Whatever is moved (changed) must be moved (changed) by another.

4 The chain of movers cannot go on to infinity (**infinite regress**), since then there would be no first mover.

5 If we trace movement back far enough we must arrive at the first mover, moved by no other.

6 According to Aquinas, this first mover is what we understand to be God.

The Second Way: the uncaused causer

This focuses on the idea of cause and effect:

1 Nothing could be the **efficient cause** of itself. The reason for this is that it would already have had to exist in order to bring itself into existence. This would be impossible.

2 Therefore, if we trace causes back far enough, there must be a first cause, caused by no other. Infinite regress is impossible since then there would be no first cause (and so no other causes).

3 According to Aquinas, this is what we understand to be God.

> **Motion** – the process by which an object acquires a new form.
>
> **Infinite regress** – a chain of events that goes backwards for ever.

> **Exam tip**
>
> The level 5 descriptor requires candidates to show 'reasonable understanding through use of relevant example(s)'. The example of a piece of wood (potentially hot) becoming hot would be a good way of explaining movement. Explain what the example illustrates, how it illustrates it and how it supports the point you are making.

> **Efficient cause** – that which causes change and motion to start or stop. In many cases, this is simply the thing that brings something about.

> **Typical mistake**
>
> Some candidates write long introductions which include a potted biography of Aquinas or a summary of all Five Ways. Avoid doing this at all costs.

> **Typical mistake**
>
> Candidates often confuse the terms 'unmoved' mover and 'uncaused causer'. In the First Way, the mover produces the various stages through which changeable things pass, and produces another state of something. In the Second Way, the causer produces the existence of the thing.

The Third Way: possibility and necessity

For Aquinas, anything that had a property is referred to as a being:

1 The world consists of **contingent beings** which at one time did not exist.

2 If everything at one time did not exist, there would have been nothing in existence, since there would be nothing that could bring anything into existence.

3 As there are contingent beings existing now, there must be something non-contingent (or **necessary beings**).

4 According to Aquinas, this is what we understand to be God.

Typical mistake

The phrase 'contingent beings' is often misunderstood by candidates who take it to refer only to human beings. Aquinas refers to anything that has a **property** as a being.

> **Contingent beings** – beings that depend upon something else for their existence. They have the property that they need not be, or could have been, different.
>
> **Necessary beings** – beings which, if they exist, cannot *not* exist; beings which are not dependent on any other for their existence.

> **Property** – nature or character.

The argument's basis in observation
Revised ☐

- Aquinas' argument appeals to events that we see and experience in the universe (change, cause, contingent beings).
- Because the argument is based on experience, it is an **a posteriori** argument and an **inductive** argument.

> **A posteriori** – after experience, derived from observed facts.
>
> **Inductive** – a process of reasoning that draws a general conclusion from specific instances. Inductive arguments offer only probabilities, not proofs.

The rejection of infinite regress
Revised ☐

Aquinas' rejection of infinite regress is essential to his argument. This principle runs through all three elements of his argument but is unpacked and explained in his Third Way:

1 Contingent beings are temporary since at some point they come into existence and at some point will go out of existence.

2 Contingent beings cannot regress infinitely as they are temporary by nature.

3 The only explanation for existence of contingent beings is a necessary being.

4 Infinite regress is to deny any final explanation.

5 The choice is between no explanation (infinite regress) and explanation (what Aquinas called God).

The need for explanation is at the heart of the argument of the mathematician and philosopher Gottfried Leibniz (1646–1716). According to Leibniz, everything has a sufficient reason (the **principle of sufficient reason**).

Typical mistake

The word 'proof' is often wrongly applied to inductive arguments. In philosophy, proof only applies to a valid and sound deductive argument. Inductive arguments lead to degrees of probability but not certainty.

Exam tip

Do not forget to include the rejection of infinite regress when presenting Aquinas' arguments.

> **Principle of sufficient reason** – there is some sort of explanation, known or unknown, for everything.

God as the first mover, first cause and necessary being

Revised

- Each of Aquinas' three arguments concludes in the existence of a being which is what he understands to be God.
- God is not one more in a line of movers or causers. God is of a totally different order and not subject to the same conditions as the universe.
- The arguments do not attempt to fill out or demonstrate the whole nature of God.
- Aquinas was compelled to conclude that the unmoved mover and uncaused causer and the necessary being must describe God.

Exam tip

When presenting Aquinas' arguments do not forget to conclude that the unmoved mover, uncaused causer and necessary being is God.

Now test yourself

Tested

1 What type of movement did Aquinas mean in the phrase 'the unmoved mover'?
2 What type of argument is Aquinas' cosmological argument – inductive or deductive? Justify your answer.
3 According to Aquinas, why does the existence of contingent beings ultimately require the existence of a necessary being?
4 Why is rejection of infinite regress central to Aquinas' argument?
5 Compile a list of what you consider to be the five key concepts of Aquinas' cosmological argument.
6 How would you reply to the question 'Who caused God?'

Answers online

Different understandings of the role of God

Remember that other forms of the cosmological argument may be used if Aquinas is not specifically mentioned in the question.

Exam tip

Exam questions can be set specifically on Aquinas' arguments. However, other forms of the argument (e.g. Kalam, William Craig) can be referred to if Aquinas is not named in the question.

God as the temporal first cause

Revised

There are two understandings of cause:

- *in fieri* – becoming, commenced but not completed
- *in esse* – in being, actually existing.

The traditional interpretation of Aquinas' argument is cause in the first sense (*in fieri*) – that is a series stretching back into the past and so having a temporal first cause. This is a cause similar to building a pond. It happens in time and there is no requirement that the builder continue to exist after the pond is built. This means that God, having begun the process, could now cease to be as it does not depend on him to complete it. Recent scholars such as Copleston and Flew have challenged this view of Aquinas' understanding of cause. They argue that Aquinas was referring to cause *in esse* that has the idea of a sustainer.

The Kalam argument

The Kalam argument is a form of the cosmological argument that is Islamic in origin and dates back to about 850CE.

It argues for a **temporal first cause**:

1 Whatever begins to exist has a cause.

2 The universe began to exist.

3 Therefore the universe has a cause.

> **Temporal first cause** – a cause that is first in time.

God as the sustainer of motion, causation and existence

Revised

Cause *in esse* has the idea of a sustainer. It is similar to the idea that the sound of music from the playing of a piano is dependent on the person who continues to play the piano. The continued existence of God is necessary for sustaining motion, causation and existence.

God's existence is necessary to sustain the existence of everything else. Everything continues to depend on God for its existence. This is called an ontological first cause.

> **Exam tip**
>
> The different ideas of cause should be discussed.

> **Typical mistake**
>
> Students forget that every exam question has a particular focus. For example, if the role of God is the focus then do not just rehearse the cosmological argument. Keep the focus where it is meant to be – the role of God.

God as the explanation of why there is something rather than nothing

Revised

- The fact that there is something needs an explanation.
- Infinite regress provides no explanation. The fact that something exists does not explain its existence.
- The principle of sufficient reason suggests the need for an explanation.
- The explanation has to be something that stands outside the entire sequence; something that does not depend upon further explanation – a God who is eternal and necessary.

> **Key quote**
>
> An event is 'fully explained when we have cited the agent, his intention that the event occur, and his basic powers' that includes his ability to bring about events of that sort.
>
> (Richard Swinburne)

Now test yourself

Tested

7 List six different understandings of the role of God.

8 Explain the difference between cause '*in fieri*' and cause '*in esse*'.

Answers online

Key criticisms of the argument and possible responses

Argument	Key criticism of argument	Possible response
Infinite regress is not possible.	The possibility of infinite regress: The **Oscillating Universe theory**. If infinite regress is not possible then who caused God?	**Big Bang theory** is preferred. God is not one more in series but something outside of sequence. The evidence leads to God having that characteristic of all actuality.

> **Oscillating Universe theory** – the theory that there has been an infinite series of expanding and contracting universes.
>
> **Big Bang theory** – the theory of an expanding universe that began as infinitely dense energy at some finite time in the past; the initial explosion that caused it to expand is called the Big Bang.

Argument	Key criticism of argument	Possible response
The universe is 'just there' – it provides no explanation.	The possibility of the universe as a 'brute fact': Rejection of principle of sufficient reason. No explanation needed – just a brute fact.	Explanation sought in every other area of enquiry. If there is explanation then it could be God. God is the explanation that requires no further explanation.
The universe must have a cause.	Because an event in the universe has a cause, it does not mean that the universe itself must therefore have a cause (fallacy of composition).	Composition is not always a fallacy (e.g. every part of a silver coin is silver, therefore the whole coin is silver).
Identity of necessary being as God.	Why should the identity of the necessary being equate to God?	Aquinas never claimed the necessary being showed the attributes of God in the Christian tradition, but it is consistent with the idea of a transcendent being.
Argument based on observation.	It draws a conclusion that goes beyond the evidence: David Hume (1711–76) argued that we could not have knowledge about concepts such as cause and necessary beings as they were not open to the empirical approach.	We distinguish between cause and coincidence. Reason also leads to knowledge.

Exam tip

Challenging a criticism can involve not just explaining why the criticism is weak or fails, but also why the alternative is more persuasive.

Key quote

'An expanding universe does not preclude a creator, but it does place limits on when he might have carried out his job!'

(Stephen Hawking)

Key quote

'The universe is just there, and that's all there is to say.'

(Bertrand Russell)

Empirical – relying on or derived from sense experience.

Now test yourself

9 State what is meant by the fallacy of composition and explain why this is an argument against the cosmological argument.

10 Explain how Hume's empirical approach is a challenge to the cosmological argument.

Answers online

Tested

Issues arising

One of the major issues arising is the extent to which the cosmological arguments are persuasive.

Does the cosmological argument prove God or show that it is reasonable to believe in God?

Revised

Here are a series of questions that you should be asking yourself as you get your head round this issue:

- What counts as 'reasonable'?
- Can the cosmological argument be proved or is it more about degrees of certainty?
- Does the cosmological argument successfully deal with infinite regress?
- Which is a more reasonable explanation of the universe – that it is 'just there' and requires no explanation or that God is the explanation as to why there is something rather than nothing? How do you decide?
- How convincing are the criticisms of the cosmological argument?
- Is 'God' the only conclusion?

The strengths and weaknesses of the cosmological argument

Revised

Strengths	Weaknesses
It gives an explanation.	Not a proof.
Science supports a beginning to the universe.	Matter could exist necessarily without God.
Criticisms fail.	Criticisms are persuasive.
Consistent with God as the explanation.	If God does not have a cause, then why should the universe also not have a cause?
Part of the **cumulative argument for God**.	The cosmological argument is not the strongest argument for the existence of God, so it does little to strengthen the cumulative argument.

Exam tip

The issues arising are questions that test evaluation skills and therefore are *not* about listing strengths and weaknesses. Rather they involve discussing the relative weightings of the strengths against the weaknesses.

Cumulative argument for God – arguments for the existence of God that do not consist of a single decisive argument and none of which has decisive force. But the cumulative case is alleged to make the existence of God probable.

The value of the argument for religious faith

Revised

This issue requires a weighing-up of the value for religious faith of the cosmological argument. Below is a list of some possible responses that need evaluating.

Case study The cosmological argument

Of value
- It gives intellectual support for belief in God.
- Only God provides explanation that requires no further explanation.
- It reveals aspects of the nature of God (e.g. unmoved mover, sustainer, necessary being).

Of limited or no value
- The argument is flawed.
- It draws conclusions that go beyond the evidence.
- It is inductive and therefore not a proof.
- Religious faith is not based on intellectual arguments.
- Proof would leave no room for faith.

Exam tip

Religious faith is sometimes used to mean an individual personal belief, or refers to 'the faith', which is the substance of what people believe.

Now test yourself

11 'Science supports a beginning to the universe.' Justify this claim and then challenge this claim.

12 List three points to support the view that the cosmological argument has no value for religious faith.

Answers online

Tested

Exam practice

(a) Explain how Aquinas' cosmological argument attempts to prove that God exists. **(30 marks)**

(b) 'The cosmological argument has more strengths than weaknesses.' To what extent do you agree? **(15 marks)**

Answers online

Online

3.2 Religious experience

The variety of religious experience

You are required to study three types of religious experience:

- visions
- conversion experiences
- mystical experiences.

These are not mutually exclusive. For example, visions and mystical experiences could be part of a conversion experience.

Visions Revised ☐

A vision can be defined as something seen other than by ordinary sight – that is, supernatural or prophetic sight experienced in sleep or ecstasy, especially one that conveys a revelation.

Type

There are different types of vision. These are as follows:

- **Group visions** – seen by more than one person. For example, Angels of Mons: during the First World War a vision of St George and a phantom bowman halted the Kaiser's troops, while others claimed angels had thrown a protective curtain around the British troops, saving them from disaster.

- **Individual visions** – seen by only one person. For example, Bernadette of Lourdes claimed to have been instructed by an apparition of the Virgin Mary to dig a hole and a healing spring would appear. The place was Lourdes.

- **Corporeal visions** – the object is external but only visible to certain people, such as appearances of angels.

- **Imaginative visions** – the image is produced in the person's imagination and has no existence external to the person, such as John's visions of strange creatures in the Book of Revelation.
  Dreams are also sometimes considered to be visions and can be categorised under this type; for example, the wise men were warned in a dream not to return to Herod (Matthew 2:12).

> Corporeal – of a material nature, physical.

Form

The form and content of visions can be very varied and may include the following:

- An image or event in which there is a message; for example, Peter's vision of the large sheet descending (Acts 10:9–16). The sheet contained all kinds of animals and reptiles and birds. A voice told Peter to kill and eat. When he refused, the voice told him that he should not call anything impure that God has made clean. Peter then realised that he could eat with a Gentile.

- Religious figures; for example, St Teresa of Avila's most famous vision was of an angel holding a long spear at the end of which was something like a fire. This seemed to pierce her heart several times and when it was withdrawn it left her 'completely afire with a great love for God'.

- Places; for example, Guru Nanak's vision of God's court in which he was escorted into God's presence and commanded to drink a cup of nectar.

- Fantastic creatures/figures; for example, Ezekiel's vision of four living creatures (Ezekiel 1:6–14). Each had a face of a man, and on the right side the face of a lion, and on the left the face of an ox; each also had the face of an eagle.

- The final judgement/end of world; for example, John's visions of final judgement in the Book of Revelation (Revelation 20:12–15). This describes the dead being judged according to what they had done. Anyone's name that was not found in the book of life was thrown into the lake of fire.

> **Exam tip**
>
> Do not narrate, but use examples to identify and discuss the features of type and form of vision.

> **Typical mistake**
>
> Because visions can be part of conversion or a mystical experience, students often do not treat visions as a separate category and are then in difficulty when a question is set on this specific type of religious experience.

Conversion

Revised

The word 'conversion' means 'to change direction' or 'to turn around'. It is a process of change that alters one's view of the world and one's personal place in it.

Type

There are various ways in which a conversion experience can be categorised, some of which may overlap:

- A unifying of the inner self – this is how the American psychologist and philosopher, William James (*The Varieties of Religious Experience*, 1902), understood conversion. He saw it in psychological terms rather than as a miraculous occurrence. The divided self was an awareness of incompleteness.

- From no religion to a faith; for example, Augustine, who became Bishop of Hippo in 395CE and was a key thinker in the development of the Christian Church. Of his conversion, Augustine says, 'As I came to the end of the sentence, it was as though the light of confidence flooded into my heart and all the darkness of doubt was dispelled.'

- From one faith to another faith; for example, Sundar Singh, who was raised as a devout Sikh. Dissatisfied with Sikhism, he sought ultimate meaning in Hinduism and Christianity. Disenchanted with both, he made to kill himself unless God revealed himself. Then he had a vision of Jesus and became an active Christian for the rest of his life.

- From faith (believing) to faith (trusting); for example, John Wesley. He was aware that he did not have the faith in Christ as a personal saviour that he saw others had. Then, in 1738, he records how he felt his heart strangely warmed: 'I did trust Christ, Christ alone, for salvation; and an assurance was given me, that he had taken away my sins, even mine …'

> **Typical mistake**
>
> Candidates often narrate long detailed accounts of actual conversions. It is far better to allude to the account and draw from it the relevant illustrations that relate to the focus of the question.

Sometimes conversions are categorised under the headings 'intellectual' and 'moral'. An example of an intellectual conversion would be C.S. Lewis, the author of the *Narnia* Chronicles and professor at Oxford. He recounts how in 1931 he walked and talked for hours with the author J.R.R. Tolkien about myth and Christianity and became convinced that Jesus was the Son of God.

Augustine is an example of a moral conversion, in that his wayward life was challenged when he read the words from Romans which exhorts the reader to abandon the works of the flesh and to be clothed with Christ.

Key features

Even though James understood the conversion only in psychological terms, he discussed a number of key features of conversion:

- Gradual or sudden – however, even sudden conversions may have had prior **subconscious** development.
- Volitional or self-surrendering – conversion might involve the giving up of the personal will, either freely (volitional) or with resistance and an internal battle (self-surrendering).
- Passive or active – either the experience comes upon someone unexpectedly without them deliberately seeking it, or someone might specifically seek a spiritual experience by going to an evangelistic meeting.
- Transforming – conversion might involve a thorough-going transformation; a new person; a new creation.

> **Exam tip**
>
> Be aware that not all the features that appear in the various lists occur in every example of a religious experience.

> **Subconscious** – part of the mind which is just below the level of consciousness and contains material of which it is possible to become aware by redirecting attention.

> **Now test yourself**
>
> 1 Choose any two examples of a vision and comment on their type and form.
> 2 Look up the account of Paul's conversion (Acts 26:9–18) and identify and explain five different features of a conversion.
> 3 Explain the difference between the conversion of Augustine and the conversion of John Wesley.
>
> Answers online
>
> Tested ☐

Mystical experiences

Revised ☐

Mysticism can be defined as an experience that alters the state of consciousness and brings people to claim a new awareness of ultimate reality. For theists, it is usually union and communion with God. For Eastern religions, it is usually a realisation of enlightenment.

Type

Robert Zaehner, who in 1952 became Professor of Eastern Religions at Oxford University, distinguishes three types:

1 **Nature** – the experience of oneness with nature. God can be experienced through the natural world as he is everywhere; for example, Alfred Lord Tennyson described his mystic experiences: 'individuality itself seemed to dissolve and fade away into boundless being'.

2 **Monistic** – the experience of one's own spirit as the Absolute, the identity of Atman and Brahman. Found more in Eastern traditions and particularly taught by eighth-century Indian sage Shankara. The goal is the realisation of one's own identity with the Absolute Reality, so that you become that Absolute.

3 **Theistic** – union or communion with a personal Lord. Theistic mystics speak about having a consciousness of being fully absorbed

> **Exam tip**
>
> It is important to show that there is diversity within mysticism (i.e. nature, monistic, theistic).

into or even identical with God. The French abbott, Bernard of Clairvaux (1090–1153) described this unification as 'mutuality of love'.

Walter Stace, a British philosopher, distinguishes two types:

1 **Extrovertive** (outward looking) – where the plurality of objects in the world is transfigured into a single living entity; for example, the psychologist Richard Bucke's experience – 'I saw that the universe is not composed of dead matter, but is, on the contrary, a living Presence.'

2 **Introvertive** (inward looking) – where a person loses their identity as a separate individual and merges slowly into the divine unity. 'It is pure unitary consciousness wherein awareness of the world and of multiplicity is completely obliterated. It is ineffable peace. It is the Supreme Good. It is One without a second. It is the Self (The Upanishads).

Key features

William James identified four features of mysticism:

1 **Ineffability** – no adequate account of the experience can be given in words. It defies expression. Phrases such as 'the dissolution of the personal ego' are empty to those who have not experienced such things.

2 **Noetic quality** – they are states that allow apparent insight into the depths of truths unobtainable by the intellect alone. They have a force of certainty and reality.

3 **Transiency** – the states cannot be maintained for long periods of time. Though the states are remembered, they are imperfectly recalled. Usually they leave the recipient with a profound sense of the importance of the experience.

4 **Passivity** – there is a sense of feeling that one is taken over by a superior power.

The philosopher F.C. Happold identified another three characteristics:

1 Consciousness of the oneness of everything – the usual awareness of identity, or ego, fades away and the person becomes aware of being part of a dimension much greater than themselves. This unity can be introvertive, where external sense impressions are left behind, or extrovertive, where the person reports that they feel a part of everything that is (i.e. all is one).

2 Sense of timelessness – the subject feels in a realm of eternity or infinity – beyond past, present and future, and beyond ordinary three-dimensional space.

3 The idea that the ego is not the real 'I' – this seems to be a sense that there is an unchanging self that is immortal and that lies behind the usual experience of self.

The Italian medieval theologian and philosopher St Bonaventure identified three stages of a mystic experience:

1 **The purgative stage** – the mystic is purified and prepared for the experience through meditation.

> **Key quote**
>
> 'The soul is fully awake as regards God, but wholly asleep as regards things of this world.'
>
> (St Teresa of Avila)

> **Exam tip**
>
> It is worth learning a few good examples which you can comment on that illustrate the various features and characteristics of religious experience.

> **Typical mistake**
>
> Candidates often tend to give lists of features without explanation. What is required are clear explanations that are then illustrated and commented on.

> **Typical mistake**
>
> Candidates learn quotes but mistakenly think that a quote without a comment will suffice as an explanation.

2 **The illuminative stage** – the mystic is affected both in his intellect and his feelings.

3 **The unitive stage** – the mystic gains a continuing union with the Divine.

The numinous

Revised

The term was coined by the German theologian Rudolf Otto (*The Idea of the Holy*, 1917). He argued that there was one common factor to all religious experience – the numinous. For Otto, religious experience is about a feeling – an experience of the holy. It is something 'wholly other' than the natural world and beyond apprehension and comprehension. He identified a number of elements:

- awe and wonder – inspiring a sort of profound unease
- overpoweringness – inspires a feeling of humility
- energy/urgency – creating an impression of immense vigour, compelling
- wholly other – totally outside normal experience
- fascination – causes the subject of the experience to be caught up in it.

A good example of the numinous is the experience of Moses at the Burning Bush (Exodus 3:6). The bush was on fire but was not consumed by the flames. It is the occasion when Moses was appointed by God to lead the Israelites out of Egypt and into the Promised Land of Canaan.

Now test yourself

4 Name five types of mystical experience.

5 List the four key features of mystic experiences identified by William James.

Answers online

Tested

Religious experience and the existence of God

If you have the experience

Revised

The heart of the argument that religious experience gives as evidence for the existence of God concerns the reliability of our sense experiences. The claim is that what one seems to experience is probably the case because we have to trust our senses, otherwise we would be sceptical about everything. There are at least two versions of this argument.

1 Alston and foundational beliefs

An American philosopher, William Alston (1921–2009), argued that belief in God from mystical experiences is justified and rational as long as there are no reasons to believe that apparent mystical perceptions are unreliable. Justification is on the grounds of:

- some mystical experiences should be regarded as perceptions of God because they are similar to the perception of physical objects in sense experience; for example, similar to touching something
- a direct encounter with (or immediate perception of) God is a foundational belief. Foundational beliefs are beliefs that are not derived from any other belief. They are self-justifying; for example, I am in pain.

2 Swinburne and the principle of credulity

Like Alston, the British philosopher Richard Swinburne argues that what someone claims to perceive is probably the case. Swinburne proposed the principle of credulity. This stated that it is reasonable to believe that the world is probably as we experience it to be (i.e. the experience is **veridical**), unless there are special reasons for thinking the experience is false. He then listed four special reasons that might cast doubt on the validity of the event:

- if the person was unreliable (e.g. drugged)
- if similar perceptions are shown to be false (e.g. drug-induced by taking LSD)
- if there is strong evidence that the object or person was not present, did not exist (e.g. a mirage)
- if the event can be accounted for in other ways (e.g. stimulating **temporal lobes** can produce a religious experience).

> **Veridical** – when what you experience actually exists as a reality and not just in your imagination.
>
> **Temporal lobes** – one of the four main lobes or regions of the cerebral cortex.

> **Exam tip**
>
> It is important to give examples to illustrate the principle of credulity. Part of the level 5 descriptor states 'showing reasonable understanding through use of relevant example(s)'.

If someone tells you about their experience

Revised

Again, the heart of the argument that religious experience gives as evidence for the existence of God concerns the reliability of our sense experiences. However, this time the focus is on when someone tells us about their experience, rather than us having the experience ourselves. Should we believe them?

There are at least three versions of this argument.

1 The inductive argument

This is an inductive argument because the conclusion does not necessarily follow from the premises. It argues that people claiming they experience God is good reason to believe that God exists:

- If an entity is experienced, then it must exist.
- People claim they experience God.
- Therefore, God probably exists.

> **Typical mistake**
>
> Candidates refer to this argument as 'proof'. This is a mistake. Inductive arguments can only provide degrees of probabilities.

2 Swinburne and the principle of testimony

Swinburne uses the principle of credulity as part of his argument to derive his principle of testimony. He argues that other people's testimony of religious experiences provides good reason to believe that God exists:

- What one seems to perceive is probably the case (principle of credulity).
- Many people, on the basis of apparent direct experiences of God, take it that God exists.
- In the absence of special considerations, it is reasonable to believe that the experiences of others are probably as they report them (principle of testimony).
- Therefore, God probably exists.

> **Exam tip**
>
> Setting out an argument in premises and conclusion (as here) makes it much easier to discuss challenges to the argument.

3 Swinburne and the cumulative argument

Another of Swinburne's arguments for the existence of God from religious experience is the **cumulative argument**, in which he concludes: 'On our total evidence theism is more probable than not.' The onus is on the sceptic to show that religious experience should be rejected, rather than for the believer to show that it is true.

> **Cumulative argument** – a collection of arguments that together increase the persuasiveness of the case.

Using his argument from principle of testimony, he develops the cumulative argument:

- On the basis of the principle of testimony, it is probable that some religious experiences are real and accurate (i.e. they are veridical).

- The claim that God exists can be defeated only if it is significantly more probable that God does not exist.

- The cumulative argument (i.e. other arguments for the existence of God such as the cosmological argument) shows that it is more probable that God exists.

- Therefore, the claim that religious experiences are real and accurate (i.e. they are veridical) is more likely to be true than the claim that they are delusive.

- Therefore, it is up to the sceptic to show that religious experiences are delusive.

Now test yourself   Tested

6   What is meant by a foundational belief?

7   What is meant by the principle of credulity?

8   Explain how the cumulative argument for the existence of God puts the onus on the sceptic to show that religious experiences are delusive.

Answers online

Challenges and possible responses

Just as the argument for religious experience as evidence for the existence of God centred on the reliability of our sense experiences, so do the challenges.

From philosophy   Revised

Challenges from philosophy involve questioning reasoning and fundamental concepts and ideas.

> **Subjective** – having its source within the mind; dependent on the subject.

The challenge	How it challenges	Possible responses
Religious experiences are not the same as sense experiences.	God is not material. God does not have a definite location. How would you recognise it was God that you were experiencing?	Just as we are known to each other by a kind of awareness and understanding of the mind rather than through our physical body, so in the same way we may be able to experience God, who is non-physical.
A direct experience of God is impossible.	The finite cannot experience the infinite. Our senses detect objects that are in time and space. God is not such an object.	It may be possible for God to enter into time and space. It is reasonable to believe that God would seek to interact with his creatures.
A religious experience cannot be verified.	A religious experience is a **subjective** event, private to the person experiencing it. Therefore, it is impossible for someone else to verify that event since they have no access to it.	Some religious experiences appear to be shared by many people. There may be criteria that would add weight to validity (e.g. the experience makes a noticeable difference to the religious life of the person). Swinburne argues that the onus is on the sceptic to show the experience is delusive.
There is a lack of uniformity of religious experiences.	The messages, visions, information and beliefs apparently transmitted in religious experiences are so diverse and contradictory that it is impossible for the majority of religious experiences to be real and accurate (e.g. Zen Buddhism claims meditation makes you fully in touch with the true nature of reality, while some Christians claim they meet with God or Jesus in their religious experience).	God may reveal himself in terms of cultural beliefs that we will understand and interpret. Different experiences recounted do not mean they are all in error. Perhaps only one religion is correct so the other religious experiences are false, but those of that one religion are true.

From science

Revised

Challenges from science involve questioning facts and explanations of facts.

The challenge	How it challenges	Possible responses
Physiological explanations	Drugs, such as hallucinogens, have been linked to religious experiences – e.g. Walter Pahnke experimented on twenty Christian theology students as they participated in an extended Good Friday religious service. Half of the participants were medicated with the hallucinogen psilocybin. The medicated group showed evidence of having increased religious experiences.	The neurological changes associated with religious experiences may mean the subject actually perceives a spiritual reality rather than the brain causing those experiences.
	Stimulation of the temporal lobes produces altered perception akin to religious experiences – e.g. Michael Persinger devised a helmet that would stimulate the temporal lobes. He claimed that it produced an experience of 'sensed presence' in over 80 per cent of test subjects. The temporal lobes could provide a natural explanation for the so-called 'religious' experiences.	Stimulating the temporal lobes may not induce the experience but facilitate it. It is difficult to isolate what is the cause and what is the effect of the experiences.
	Brain imaging shows that certain regions of the brain are active during religious experiences, which may account for the various aspects of the experience – e.g. Andrew Newberg studied the brains of Franciscan nuns during prayer, Tibetan monks during meditation, and Pentecostals speaking in tongues. The brain activity was similar in each case.	The neurological changes associated with religious experiences may mean the subject actually perceives a spiritual reality rather than that the brain is causing those experiences.
	Isolation and sensory deprivation may explain religious experiences of holy men living in some sort of wilderness.	Deprivation may help to 'fine-tune' our spiritual awareness.
Psychological explanations	Personality traits – feeling rather than thinking is typical of the religious. Therefore, a particular personality trait will be likely to be drawn to religious belief.	Religious believers have all types of personality traits.
	Carl Jung said the source of religious experience is the psyche. Part of our psyche contains structures that are image-creating. These are called archetypes. The God archetype generates religious images. A religious experience is an indirect encounter with the God archetype.	Jung's theory of archetypes can be more simply explained by the fact that all human beings share similar experiences.

Exam practice answers at **www.therevisionbutton.co.uk/myrevisionnotes**

Now test yourself

Tested

9 Explain what is meant by saying that religious experiences are subjective events.

10 Why does lack of uniformity of religious experiences challenge the reliability of religious experiences?

Answers online

Issues arising

One of the major issues arising is whether the claimed occurrences of religious experience show the existence of God. It may be more persuasive to believe that God exists for the individual who has the experience than for someone being told about the experience.

Can religious experience show that God probably exists?

Revised

For	Against
It is rational to believe (Alston and foundational beliefs).	There is no God.
The onus of proof is on the sceptic (Swinburne).	Subjective experiences cannot be verified.
The challenges from philosophy and science are flawed.	Natural explanations can never be ruled out.
The weight of the evidence in terms of numbers of people claiming a religious experience makes it unlikely that they are all delusions.	The challenges from philosophy and science are successful.
Some experiences appear to be shared by many people (e.g. **Toronto blessing**).	

Toronto blessing – a phenomenon said to have occurred at Toronto Airport Vineyard Church in 1994, in which many of the congregation fell to the ground, shook, wept or laughed uncontrollably. It was interpreted as an outpouring of the Holy Spirit.

Is it necessary to have a religious experience to understand what a religious experience is?

Revised

For	Against
The problem of ineffability – the experiences are beyond verbal description. There are no words that can describe the experience, so it is not possible for others to understand.	The ability to categorise religious experiences and identify key features means that it is possible to understand what a religious experience is.
The experience is subjective and private – it is not open to anyone else.	Some religious experiences have objective features, such as speaking in tongues.
The experience is personal – it is not possible to fully understand unless we have the experience. We cannot understand that which is beyond our own experiences.	Science has given us insight into religious experiences, such as showing what happens in the brain and so what that might indicate about the experience the person is having.

Are the challenges to religious experience successful?

This issue requires a weighing-up of the success, or failure, of the arguments and responses listed on page 92. Ask yourself some key questions, for example:

- If there is a God, why doesn't he reveal himself to everyone, especially if he wants us to believe in him?
- Although some claimed religious experiences might be explained by natural causes, is it reasonable to think that *all* claimed religious experiences are wrong?
- Richard Dawkins tried the Persinger helmet and he claimed it did not produce any sensation of a religious experience. So what conclusion can be drawn? Does it weaken or strengthen the challenge to religious experience?

Now test yourself

Tested ☐

11 Explain how the example of Persinger's helmet might be used to challenge religious experiences as an argument for the existence of God.

Answer online

Exam practice

(a) Examine the main characteristics of (i) conversion and (ii) mystical experiences. **(30 marks)**

(b) 'It is not necessary to have a religious experience in order to understand fully what a religious experience is.'
How far do you agree? **(15 marks)**

Answers online

Online ☐

3.3 Psychology and religion

One issue that the psychology of religion explores is the extent to which religious belief is a product of the human mind. Two key psychologists who investigated and commented on this particular issue were Sigmund Freud (1856–1939) and Carl Jung (1875–1961).

Freud and his understanding of religion

The heart of Freud's understanding of religion is in his theory of repression. In 1900, he wrote *The Interpretation of Dreams*, in which he argued that dreams are disguised fulfilments of wishes that are repressed by the consciousness (ego) and are displaced into the unconsciousness. Later, Freud concluded that these repressed wishes intrude into everyday life, as in small slips of the tongue ('Freudian slips'), dreams and certain neurotic symptoms.

A collective neurosis Revised

When Freud observed his mentally ill patients who had **neurosis**, he compared their behaviour to religious behaviour:

- hysterical behaviour – sometimes seen in worship (a recent example might be the phenomenon known as the '**Toronto blessing**')
- phobias and anxieties – a possible explanation for beliefs (for example, the hope of heaven/forgiveness and fear of judgement/damnation/hell)
- obsessive behaviour – similar to certain religious rituals (for example, the celebration of Holy Communion that involves a complicated ritual of actions).

Freud concluded that religion is an outward expression of inner psychological conflict. This conflict is an imbalance in the personality that is reflected in certain neurotic behaviour. He saw religion as a **collective neurosis**.

> **Neurosis** – any sort of physical behaviour or symptom that has no physical cause but a cause that is rooted in the mind.
>
> **Toronto blessing** – a phenomenon said to have occurred at Toronto Airport Vineyard Church in 1994 in which many of the congregation fell to the ground, shook, wept or laughed uncontrollably. It was interpreted as an outpouring of the Holy Spirit.
>
> **Collective neurosis** – a neurotic illness that afflicts all people.

The origins of collective neurosis-the primal horde Revised

In 1913 Freud wrote *Totem and Taboo*, in which he sought to explain the origins of religion in human beings:

- The evolutionary biologist Charles Darwin had conjectured that human beings had originally lived in small 'hordes' or groups.
- Freud speculated that the horde was dominated by one powerful and violently jealous male who had seized the women for himself and had driven off or killed all rivals, including his sons.
- The young males then united, and together they killed the dominant father so they could become dominant over the horde and gain wives themselves.

> **Key quote**
>
> 'Religion is the universal obsessional neurosis of humanity.'
>
> (Sigmund Freud)

- After the event, the young males felt guilty for they had both loved and feared the father. Moreover, with their father's death they had become rivals among themselves for the possession of the women.
- Burdened with guilt and faced with the imminent collapse of their social order, the brothers formed a tribe and a totem took the place of the father, so uniting the tribe.
- The totem was usually an animal and became worshipped. It was taboo to kill the totem animal. A memory of these events was inherited by later generations. It was commemorated each year by a ritual killing and eating of the totem animal.
- This act of ritual killing also reflected the belief that rituals and actions could control objects and living things.

> **Exam tip**
>
> Remember not to confuse assessment objectives. AO1 for 30 marks asks you to examine, explain or outline, but not to assess or evaluate. Therefore, when asked to explain Freud's understanding of religion do not include a criticism of it.

Freud postulated that this sequence of events was a condensed form of what must have happened countless times over thousands of years. He argued that each succeeding generation down to the present has inherited the sense of guilt resulting from having killed the father or having entertained such thoughts. Freud maintained that the Christian doctrine of **atonement** represents a particularly undisguised reflection of this event.

> **Atonement** – making up for wrongdoing; the reconciliation of man with God through life, sufferings and the sacrificial death of Christ.

The table below shows some possible parallels.

Christian doctrine of atonement	Link with primal horde theory
Christ gave up his own life to redeem us from the burden of original sin.	It implies the original sin was murder.
The outcome of Christ's death was reconciliation with God the Father.	It implies that this original sin was not just murder but murder of the father.
Christ now replaces the father as the centre of religious devotion through his offering of atonement.	Reflection of the positive and negative feelings of the sons towards the father.
Holy Communion is a symbolic ritual and remembrance.	The totemic meal. Identifying with the son.

Now test yourself — Tested ☐

1 According to Freud, what event did the eating of the totem animal represent?

Answer online

The Oedipus complex — Revised ☐

Many people find Freud's explanation of the primal horde unconvincing as an account of the origin in human beings of the connection between the father complex and belief in God. Freud's theory of the **Oedipus complex** provides a more convincing account of the origins of this father complex and belief in God in the individual.

Freud believed that the sexual drive (libido) was the most basic urge. Therefore, it was the urge most capable of causing major psychological problems. The libido is seen by Freud as not just the desire to have sex but represents the body's **subconscious** desire for satisfaction that originates in the unconscious.

He argued that young boys between the ages of four and seven have a kind of love affair with their mothers. As the son develops, he sees his

> **Oedipus complex** – the theory that young boys are sexually attracted to their mothers but resent their fathers. The feelings are repressed as they fear the father. Oedipus refers to a character in a Greek legend that unwittingly killed his father and married his own mother.
>
> **Subconscious** – part of the mind which is just below the level of consciousness and contains material of which it is possible to become aware by redirecting attention.

father as a rival for his mother's attentions and affections. He wants to replace his father but fears him. In particular, he fears genital mutilation. Three factors conspire to make the young boy fear this:

- He has already experienced the loss of his mother's breasts, which he thought were part of his own body.
- He has been threatened with the loss of his penis when a parent discovered him manipulating it.
- He has discovered that there are human beings without a penis – not realising it is because they are female but thinking it is punishment for having forbidden desires.

The conflict of frustration, guilt and anguish is repressed and hidden in the subconscious. The only way that this is eventually given release is through neurotic symptoms.

Freud was struck by the parallels to the Greek legend of Oedipus and so named this the Oedipus complex.

Similarities between the theories

The same features of the desire to eliminate the father and the wish to possess the mother are the basis of both the primal horde theory and the Oedipus complex theory. Each seeks to explain the resulting neurotic behaviour expressed through the belief and practices of religion.

The analogous stage for girls to the Oedipus complex is known as the Electra complex, in which girls feel desire for their fathers and jealousy of their mothers.

> **Key quote**
>
> 'We recognise that the roots for the need for religion are in the parental complex.'
>
> (Sigmund Freud)

> **Key quote**
>
> 'The super-ego retains the character of the father, while the more powerful the Oedipus complex was and the more rapidly it succumbed to repression (under the influence of authority, religious teaching, schooling and reading), the stricter will be the domination of the super-ego over the ego later on – in the form of conscience or perhaps of an unconscious sense of guilt.'
>
> (Sigmund Freud)

> **Now test yourself**   Tested
>
> 2 According to Freud, why does the Oedipus complex give rise to neurotic symptoms?
>
> 3 What is meant by the Electra complex?
>
> Answers online

Freud's view of religion as collective neurosis   Revised

Freud's view was that there were two universal sources of religious ideas:

1 The unconscious **racial memories** of the slaughter of the primal father.

2 The early childhood experiences of our own parents – the Oedipus complex.

However, this view of Freud has not been unchallenged:

- Darwin's theory about hordes has been challenged. Some think that there was a much greater variety of structure within the earliest groups and tribes.
- There is no evidence that the primal horde crime ever occurred.
- There is no evidence that guilt can be transmitted in the way that Freud argues.
- Freud had been influenced by writings of his day which argued that the essence of religion was sacred actions and rites rather than a set

> **Racial memories** – a supposedly inherited subconscious memory of events in human history or prehistory.

of beliefs or doctrines. This approach no longer holds sway in the academic world.

- Freud's approach to the origins of religion predated his study of religions. He selected the evidence that fitted his theory. Freud wrote in a letter about his reading of books on religion: 'I am reading books without being really interested in them, since I already know the results; my instinct tells me that.'

- Freud's theory concerning the origins of religion in the individual is incapable of being tested. It is a **hypothesis**, not a fact. Where it can be tested it has generally been shown to be wrong.

- Freud argued that the Oedipus complex accounted for people modelling God on their father. However, some research suggests that most people tend to model God on their mother.

- The Polish anthropologist Bronislaw Malinowski studied the Trobriand race and found no evidence of the Oedipus complex, although they had a religion. He concluded that the complex does not cause the religion – rather the religion, with its strict rules on sexual behaviour and relationships, causes the Oedipus complex that then leads to the neurosis.

> **Typical mistake**
>
> Often candidates mistakenly write about the Oedipus complex when asked about Jung, and write about archetypes when answering a question on Freud. It is vital that you link the correct theory with the correct psychologist.

> **Hypothesis** – a suggested explanation.

> **Now test yourself**
>
> 4   Identify three challenges to the primal horde theory.
>
> **Answer online**
>
> Tested ☐

A wish fulfilment

Revised ☐

Freud's ideas were influenced heavily by the philosopher Ludwig Feuerbach, who saw God as a 'projection' of the human mind based on human longings and desires. In *The Future of an Illusion* (1927), Freud outlined his idea of religion as an 'illusion' based on wish fulfilment of the deepest yearnings and longings of the human unconscious. This re-emphasised the personal origin of religion. The Christian religion provides examples of wish fulfilment through religion. These include the idea of a 'father figure', Jesus the healer and miracle worker, answered prayers and God as all powerful, all knowing and all loving.

> **Key quote**
>
> 'Religion was an attempt to get control over the sensory world, in which we are placed, by means of the wish world, which we have developed inside us as a result of biological and psychological necessities.'
>
> (Sigmund Freud)

A reaction against helplessness

Revised ☐

Religion helps us deal with suffering and helplessness through the illusion of authority presented in religion by a God who needs to be obeyed. Two examples:

- Aggression, which can be dysfunctional, can be controlled by religious teaching that seeks to limit war and violence.

- The sexual drive can be controlled through the strict religious laws governing sexual ill behaviour and relationships. This strong drive can also be redirected into charity work, which can be seen as service to God. Obedience and unselfish work for others can be seen in the **parable of the sheep and the goats**. Those that obey and serve will be rewarded with heaven.

Another area of helplessness is the fear of the forces of nature, including death. We need to be able to be in control. Religion allows an outlet for this wish fulfilment (of being in control) through the illusion of power presented in religion by an omnipotent God. Two examples:

> **Key quote**
>
> 'Freud's atheism was the presupposition, not the outcome, of his theories.'
>
> (Alister McGrath, philosopher and theologian)

> **Parable of the sheep and the goats** – the parable teaches that on the Day of Judgement the secret motives of the heart will be revealed. People will reap what they have sown and those who have failed to perform good deeds will face judgement.

- Natural forces are not seen as impersonal. God is the controller of nature. Prayer can overcome illness and avert natural disasters. Even with natural disasters, God is still seen to be ultimately control.
- The fear of death is overcome by the promise of life after death.

Now test yourself

Tested

5 Give an example of how religion helps us to deal with suffering and helplessness through (a) the illusion of authority, (b) the illusion of power.

Answer online

Jung and his understanding of religion

In contrast with Freud, Jung did not think that religion was a neurosis, but saw it as something necessary for personal growth. He agreed with Freud about the personal unconscious that consisted of lost or repressed memories, some of which take the form of complexes. However, below the individual unconscious, Jung claimed lies the **collective unconscious**.

Collective unconscious – a part of the unconscious mind incorporating patterns of memories, instincts and experiences common to all human beings.

An expression of the collective unconscious

Revised

According to Jung, the collective unconscious consists of **primordial** images derived from the early prehistory of the race, rather like instincts. In studying the dreams and fantasies of his patients, Jung discovered ideas and images whose origin could not be traced to the individual's own past experiences. The resemblance of these dreams and fantasies to mythical and religious themes which have appeared throughout the world led Jung to refer to them as primordial images or **archetypes**.

Primordial – the earliest, or relating to an early stage of development.

Archetypes – symbolic forms which all people share in their collective unconscious. The archetypes give rise to images in the conscious mind and account for the reoccurring themes in myths and fairy tales as well as in dreams.

The theory of archetypes

Revised

Archetypes are not created; rather they are discovered in the collective unconscious. They are limitless in number and finding new archetypes is a matter of searching deep within one's self to discover them. Although they are limitless in number, there are a few particularly notable, recurring archetypal images that Jung identified which exhibited regular patterns of meaning. Archetypes cannot be known directly but they generate images in the conscious mind which are derived from culture and personal experience. Jung saw them as images of the dominant laws and principles which are responsible for the human quality of human beings. They possess emotional force and are images of typical, regularly occurring events in the soul's cycle of experience.

Some of the key archetypes that Jung identified are as follows:

The persona

This is the mask we wear to make a particular impression on others and it may also conceal our own true nature. The persona represents all of the different social masks that we wear among different groups and in different situations.

The shadow

This is the suppressed, unconscious part of the personality, symbolised by the devil, a snake or original sin. It is in contrast to the persona, which is the public self. We deny in ourselves this darker side of our personality. The unrecognised shadow is projected upon others who are thought to embody the repressed tendencies that are actually resident in an individual's own **psyche**.

Anima and animus

These are our inner attitudes that take on the characteristics of the opposite sex. The anima is the archetypal image of woman present in the unconscious of every man. It is responsible for moods and is a complication in all emotional relationships. The comparable archetype in the female psyche is the animus, the woman's image of man. In the woman's unconscious, it is responsible for unreasoned opinion.

The Self

This is the most important archetype and is the midpoint of the personality – midway between consciousness and the unconscious. It signifies the harmony and balance of the various opposing qualities that constitute the psyche. Because it is virtually impossible for any person to embody the Self fully, this archetype is often expressed by abstract or geometrical forms (e.g. the **mandala**). Prominent human figures that express the Self are the Buddha and Christ. The Self could also be considered a symbol of what religions call the 'soul'.

> **Psyche** – the totality of the human mind, conscious and unconscious.

> **Exam tip**
>
> There are a number of technical terms that might appear in the exam question, for example: archetype, the Self. It is important that you understand them and use them appropriately.

> **Key quote**
>
> 'The concept of the archetype … indicates the existence of definite forms in the psyche which seem to be present always and everywhere.'
>
> (Carl Jung)

> **Mandala** – geometric designs symbolic of the universe, often used in Hinduism and Buddhism as an aid to meditation.

> **Now test yourself** | Tested

6 Explain what Jung meant by an 'archetype'.

7 What archetype is often symbolised by (a) a snake, (b) the mandala?

Answers online

The 'god within' | Revised

It was important for Jung that people did not see the idea of God as Freud did – that is, as created by the individual human mind and its neurotic desires. For Jung, God is a deep 'inner' reality but not an external object or person. God is an expression of the collective unconscious. An encounter with the Self is a 'religious experience' with God. The experience is 'spiritual' or 'numinous'. The German theologian Rudolf Otto described a 'numinous' experience as mysterious and awe-inspiring, during which the person feels to be in communion with a 'wholly other'.

Jung argued that the Self archetype produced the same symbolism that has always expressed the deity. He claimed that it was impossible to distinguish between a symbol of the Self and a God image. The Self, Jung concluded, is the 'God within us'.

> **Key quote**
>
> 'Too few people have experienced the divine image as the innermost possession of their own souls. Christ only meets them from without, never from within the soul.'
>
> (Carl Jung)

The quest for integration and the process of individuation | Revised

The process by which a person moves toward the achievement of the Self is called **individuation**. It involves the integration into consciousness of

> **Individuation** – the process of attaining wholeness and balance.

the various diverse contents of the unconscious by means of archetypal symbols. The integration results in wholeness and balance of an individual's personality. The Self archetype works collectively with all other aspects of a person's psyche to integrate them and become whole. It is a form of 'self-development', 'self-realisation' or a 'discovery of the true self or of our true nature'.

The aim of individuation is to divest the Self of the false wrappings of the persona and the suggestive power of the primordial images – to balance the contradictory nature of the archetypes and unite opposites. For instance, we need to unite good and evil and try to see ourselves as capable of both. Eastern religions often symbolise this with the lotus, which has its roots in the dirty mud below and its flower in the clean air above.

According to Jung, one must get in touch with the shadow and anima/animus before one can truly get in touch with the Self. The symbols of the archetypes are the means by which the archetypes are brought into our consciousness from the collective unconscious. They mediate the process of individuation and these images are none other than the images that make up the religious traditions. Jung argued that only by living in harmony with the primordial images of the unconscious, by bringing our thinking into agreement with them, can we live life fully.

Individuation is the journey towards becoming a full individual. It is the quest to find the 'God within' and the symbol of 'the Self'. In its widest sense it is a religious quest, because it is through religious images that the personality achieves its goal of integration. The religious images are simply images of the deeper self.

> **Key quote**
>
> '… religion excels all rationalistic systems in that it alone relates to the outer and inner man in equal degree.'
>
> (Carl Jung)

Examples of the process of individuation from religion

Revised

Religion as an expression of the collective unconscious through the process of individuation can be seen in Buddhist meditation. Meditation is an ancient practice that existed long before the time of the Buddha. In essence, it is a form of deep concentration and analysis that explores the processes of the mind and its relationship to the physical world.

Some people might see Jung's ideas about the process of individuation at work within Buddhist meditation. The first four archetypes (persona, shadow, anima, animus) are all to do with uncovering misconceptions about who and what we are. In Buddhist meditation, removal of ignorance is vital; this involves removal of hindrances (for example, sensuous desires, ill-will, restlessness). The God archetype is directly connected to the development of positive, wholesome images for reflection, which is similar to Buddhist meditation, for example **the Brahma Viharas**. The idea of the Self archetype organising and harmonising the 'fuller picture' of reality is similar to the idea of meditation leading to enlightenment (nibbana/nirvana).

Similarly, in Christianity, 'practising the presence of Christ' in the contemplative tradition has parallels with meditation.

> **The Brahma Viharas** – the four boundless states of loving kindness, compassion, altruistic joy and composure.

> **Now test yourself**
>
> 8 Why can the quest for integration be seen as a religious quest?
>
> Answer online
>
> Tested

The challenge to religion and religious response

The theories of both Freud and Jung challenge some religious thinking and religious thinkers have responded to these challenges.

	The challenge to religion	Religious response
Freud	Religion is a neurosis – a mental illness and is therefore harmful.	Religion is positive and of value to many.
	Explains away God – wish fulfilment, Oedipus complex.	Religion claims to have evidence for an external God (e.g. Jesus' **resurrection**).
	Religion will eventually die out and be replaced by science.	Freud's theories have flaws (e.g. there is no evidence that the primal horde crime ever occurred).
	God did not create human beings; human beings created God.	There is no evidence that religion is dying out.
		Atheism can also be psychologically explained.
Jung	God is seen as an inner psychological experience – not an external being.	Religion claims to have evidence for an external God (e.g. Jesus' resurrection).
	Archetypes explain the origin of the God image.	Jung's theories have flaws (e.g. uniform images are explained by uniform experiences rather than archetypes).
	Rejects the idea of a relationship with God.	Religions have major differences between themselves.
	Religion is about the process of individuation.	Jung's theories are unverifiable (e.g. it cannot be demonstrated that there is a collective unconscious which contains the archetypes).
		Jung does not explain atheism.

Now test yourself   Tested ☐

9 State three ways in which Freud attempts to explain away God.
10 What is Jung's understanding of God?
11 Why is atheism a problem for Freud's view?

Answers online

> **Resurrection** – to come back from the dead

Issues arising

One of the major issues arising is the extent to which psychology has explained away God.

Has 'God' been explained away by psychology?   Revised ☐

As with all the issues arising, there is not a clear 'yes' or 'no' answer. It depends which psychologist is being considered. Here we look at Freud and Jung as examples. For further critiques of Freud's theories, see pages 97–98.

Freud

Freud seems to explain God away. God is a creation of the mind triggered by wish fulfilment or neurosis (primordial horde and Oedipus complex). He viewed religion as a mental illness. It was something that needed to be cured. Freud believed that with the advance of science, religion would eventually die out.

However, Freud did not claim that his theories disproved the existence of God. Even if mankind created the idea of God out of fear and guilt, this would not prove that God does not exist.

Jung

Jung seems more positive than Freud about the idea of God. For Jung, to have a religious outlook was not about subscribing to a particular creed or belonging to a religious organisation. He wrote about the 'god within', referring to a deep inner reality. Some would equate this with the postmodernist view of religion. For Jung, to experience the archetype of the Self was seen as a religious experience.

However, many would argue that an experience which stems from the mind, and as such is in no way external to the subject, cannot be termed religious. Many religious believers would argue that Christ, for example, is more than just a symbol for something else. Rather, he is a historical person and the Son of God. Therefore, it seems that Jung did not believe in the existence of God in the traditional sense of an external being. Indeed, he thought that we can never know whether God exists.

Exam practice answers at **www.therevisionbutton.co.uk/myrevisionnotes**

The strengths and weaknesses of psychological views of religion

Revised ☐

This requires you to weigh up how strong or weak the various arguments are. This means discussing how persuasive they are, rather than just stating what the arguments are. The various arguments and responses can be found on pages 95–102.

Take, for example, Freud's theory about the primal horde and totems. Some may argue that this is a weak attempt to explain the origins of the Christian doctrine of atonement. It is weak because Darwin's theory about hordes has been challenged by those who think that there was a much greater variety of structure within the earliest groups and tribes. Also, there is no evidence that the primal horde crime ever occurred or that guilt can be transmitted in the way that Freud advocates.

On the other hand, the theory is consistent with some research into primate behaviour and some anthropological findings about tribes that eat their totem animal, which symbolises God. This theory does also give an interpretation of religious sacrifice.

Exam tip

Remember that weighing up involves evaluation and not just reciting the arguments.

Now test yourself

Tested ☐

12 'Jung has a positive view of religion.' Give one argument to support this view and one argument to challenge this view.

Answer online

What is the relationship between religion and mental health?

Revised ☐

Jung's theory sees religion as being helpful to balance mental health and sees religion as a key to the process of integration and individuation. In contrast, Freud's theories see religion as unhelpful to balanced mental health. Religion is seen as a neurosis, a mental illness, and therefore something that needs to be cured. However, even Freud did see positive aspects of religion in terms of coping with fear of natural forces, including death.

Fundamentalists – religious believers who follow a strict adherence to the fundamental principles of any set of beliefs. Sometimes they are characterised as being intolerant of other views.

Revivalist services – religious services held in order to inspire members of a Church or to gain new converts.

Positive relationship between religion and mental health	Negative relationship between religion and mental health
Research by the sociologist Rodney Stark (1971) concluded that those who never go to church or have no religion are more likely to be mentally disturbed.	Some argue that being religious is in itself a sign of mental disturbance.
It seems that many religious believers have high self-esteem. Though religious believers may feel guilty and worry about sin, this is offset by believing in a loving and forgiving God.	Some psychiatric patients are religious. Their illness has taken a religious form.
Some religious believers seem to be able to cope better with the stress caused by uncontrollable life events, such as death and serious illness, which may otherwise produce depression. The psychologist Daniel McIntosh (1993) studied cases of individuals who had experienced the sudden death of a child. It was found that regular church attenders reported more social support and found meaning in their loss.	Successful religious leaders and gurus have often had a period of near-insanity. Some sects have made their members commit suicide. In the 1970s the Heaven's Gate cult based their belief system on a combination of Christian ideas of the apocalypse and elements of science fiction. Their founder, Marshall Applewhite, and 38 of his followers committed suicide in order to abandon their terrestrial forms and gain access to the UFO that they believed was trailing the comet Hale-Bopp.
Fundamentalists tend to be optimistic and benefit from the certainty of their beliefs.	Some fundamentalists tend to be dogmatic, prejudiced and have strong guilt feelings.
The suicide rate of church members is lower than for others.	Charismatic and fundamentalist **revivalist services** can be emotionally disturbing.

Exam practice

(a) Explain why Jung's understanding of religious belief may be seen as more positive than that of Freud. **(30 marks)**

(b) To what extent has religion been successful in response to psychology's challenges to religious belief? **(15 marks)**

Answers online

Online ▢

Now test yourself

13 Explain how fundamentalists may provide evidence to support the view that there is (a) a positive relationship between religion and mental health, (b) a negative relationship between religion and health.

Answer online

Tested ▢

3.4 Atheism and postmodernism

The rise of atheism

Atheism comes from the Greek word meaning 'without god', and describes the position of those who reject belief in God or gods. There are various shades of atheism ranging from antitheism (active opposition to theism) to negative atheism (no belief in God but does not assert that there is no God).

It was not really until the period of the **Enlightenment**, which began in the middle of the seventeenth century, that open atheism was made possible by the advance of religious toleration. Even then it was dangerous to deny the existence of God openly. A consequence of the Enlightenment was that human reason and the scientific method were seen as the means of finding truth.

> **Enlightenment** – the period of philosophy in the eighteenth century renowned for its emphasis on reason.

Reasons for the rise of atheism
Revised ☐

There are many reasons for a growth in the number of people believing that there is no God.

Science

The theologian Alister McGrath in *The Twilight of Atheism* (2004) gives three reasons why science was influential in the rise of atheism:

1   Science can be seen as something that frees us from bondage to a superstitious and oppressive past, i.e. religion.
2   Science is seen by some as rational while religion is seen as being irrational and full of mystery.
3   The Darwinian **theory of evolution** (see Chapter 4.2) has seemingly made belief in God unnecessary.

Darwin's theory of **natural selection** showed nature as a battleground. Prior to Darwin's theory, William Paley's book (*Natural Theology*) about the design argument (see Chapter 4.3) had been very influential. Paley had argued that nature was a mechanism and hence intelligently designed. God had created all things good and hence they required no modifications. This seemed to conflict with Darwin's theory, which was supported by evidence. People began to require evidence for belief. Those who had faith now had to defend their position.

Where previously God had been the explanation for things that could not be explained, science began to provide answers in terms of natural explanations. The **God of the gaps** began to become more and more redundant as science progressed.

Empiricism

Empiricism is the view that sense experience is the ultimate source of all our concepts and knowledge. It emphasises the role of experience and

> **Theory of evolution** – the theory that groups of organisms change with the passage of time, mainly as a result of natural selection.
>
> **Natural selection** – a key mechanism of evolution. It is the principle by which each slight variation, if useful, is preserved and the trait passed on to the next generation.
>
> **God of the gaps** – gaps in scientific knowledge are taken to be evidence or proof of God's existence.
>
> **Empiricism** – the view that experience, especially of the senses, is the only source of knowledge.

evidence, especially sensory perception, in the formation of ideas. Indeed, knowledge is restricted to what can be known by sense experience. Empiricism is an important aspect of the scientific approach and the implications for religious belief were significant. Such an approach to knowledge led to scepticism about God. God was not open to investigation by means of the senses. God is not a physical object.

Evil and suffering

The philosopher and mathematician Rene Descartes (1596–1650) supported the new age of science. Descartes wished to find certainty and in order to do so he tried to prove the existence of God. However, in trying to do this through reason alone, he failed to convince many that the case for God was certain. In addition, he unintentionally drew people's attention to an age-old problem – the problem of evil. God has the means (power) and the motivation (love, goodness) to eliminate evil and suffering. Yet evil and suffering continue in the world. For many people it raised doubts about the existence of God. The conclusion of some was that God is either limited in power, or indifferent to suffering. This caused some to reject God.

Objection to moral absolutes

Religious revelation has often been regarded as a source of authority for knowing what is right and wrong. If a system of morality is seen as being ordained by God, it can therefore be seen as absolutely binding. The laws of God are moral absolutes and they must be obeyed because God has commanded them. This view of being obligated to obey is called the Divine Command theory.

The rejection of moral absolutes therefore challenges the need for God as the source of authority. Moral absolutes are often fundamental to the teaching of a religion. As societies and cultures developed, they questioned religious views on such issues as abortion, homosexuality and assisted euthanasia. The religious revelation and the religious texts that contained the moral absolutes came into question. Morality was no longer seen to require God and so a reason for believing in God collapsed.

Awareness of other faiths

Through increased travel and communication, people became aware of other religions. As a result, it seemed that there were contradictions between the religions. They said different and incompatible things about the nature of ultimate reality and the modes of divine activity, and about the nature and destiny of the human race. Which is the word of God – the Bible or the Qur'an or the Bhagavad Gita? If what Hinduism says is true, must not what Christianity says be largely false? It was argued that which religion you follow largely depends on where you are born. It has little to do with truth.

The death of God

> **Key quote**
>
> 'It is impossible to think of a command without also thinking of the commander.'
>
> (Cardinal John Henry Newman)

> **Exam tip**
>
> Remember to explain each point that you make in an exam answer. Think carefully about each sentence and how it relates to the question and the previous sentence.

> **Key quote**
>
> 'It is a short step from the thought that the different religions cannot all be true, although they all claim to be, to the thought that in all probability none of them is true.'
>
> (John Hick, philosopher)

> **Key quote**
>
> 'If I had been born in India, I would probably be a Hindu; if in Egypt, probably a Muslim; if in Sri Lanka, probably a Buddhist; but I was born in England and am, predictably, a Christian.'
>
> (John Hick)

> **Typical mistake**
>
> It is a mistake to go in to an exam with pre-prepared essays. It will result in writing an essay that is different to the one asked for on the question paper. It may only be a bit different but it will result in your answer drifting from the focus and having parts that are irrelevant.

Origin of the slogan 'God is dead' ———————————————— Revised ☐

The phrase 'God is dead' was invented by the German philosopher Friedrich Nietzsche (1844–1900). It appears in his book *The Gay Science* (1882).

The phrase is used in a parable about a madman who goes running through a marketplace carrying a lighted lantern on a bright morning shouting, 'I seek God! I seek God!' People laugh and do not take him seriously. 'Maybe he took an ocean voyage?' some of the people suggest. In frustration, the madman smashes his lantern on the ground, crying out 'God is dead, and we have killed him, you and I. All of us are his murderers. But I have come too soon.'

The madman realises that the people cannot yet see that they have killed God. Previously God was relied upon to give the world order and meaning. However, God is now replaced by science and philosophy. God is redundant and is no longer a source of received wisdom. The new authority is science.

Implications for religion and morality
Revised

Nietzsche was aware that 'the death of God' had implications for morality. It meant the rejection of belief in an objective and universal moral law that is binding upon everyone. It meant the rejection of moral absolutes.

He believed that the majority of people did not recognise (or refused to acknowledge) this death out of fear. Therefore, when the death of God did begin to become widely acknowledged, people would despair.

Nietzsche saw that his task was to avoid this despair by re-evaluating the foundations of human values. He saw the concept of God as the greatest obstacle to the fulfilment of human life. With the death of God, people could start to acknowledge the value of this world rather than always looking towards the supernatural realm for meaning. In a godless universe, human beings would be free to create their own meanings and interpretations. These ideas were the seeds of a philosophical view known as **existentialism**. According to Nietzsche, the people who eventually learn to create their lives anew would represent a new stage in human existence, the ***Übermensch*** (the new 'super' man).

> **Existentialism** – a philosophical movement which emphasises individual existence, freedom and choice. People exist and in that existence define themselves and the world.
>
> ***Übermensch*** – in Nietzsche's philosophy, a superior human being who makes his own values and guides others.

Key quote

'When one gives up the Christian faith, one polls the right to Christian morality out from under one's feet.'

(Friedrich Nietzsche)

Key quote

'"Dead are all the Gods." It is not just one morality that has died, but all of them, to be replaced by the life of the *Übermensch*, the new man.'

(Friedrich Nietzsche)

Key quote

'God is dead: but as the human race is constituted, there will perhaps be caves for millenniums yet, in which people will show his shadow. And we – we have still to overcome his shadow!'

(Friedrich Nietzsche)

The Death of God movement
Revised

The 1960s saw the appearance of a theological movement (later dubbed 'the Death of God movement') which argued that the traditional view of God as 'out there' was no longer tenable. God has no 'real', objective or empirical existence, outside of human language. God is a potent symbol.

In Britain, these views were made popular by an Anglican bishop, John Robinson, in his book *Honest to God* (1963). He thought of God as 'the ground of our being' rather than an objective personal force. Whereas traditional theistic concepts placed God outside and above the world,

Robinson placed God deep in the human person. He argued that we need to look within to find God. For instance, whenever we pray we are not speaking words into the heavens whereby we feel relieved from responsibility from taking action ourselves. According to Robinson, our prayers should change us so we do act. This action is an expression of love and compassion, the 'ground of our being'.

In the 1980s, Don Cupitt, an Anglican priest and Dean of Emmanuel College, Cambridge, presented a TV series called '**Sea of Faith**', in which he charted the transition of some from a traditional belief in God to a rejection of a supernatural world – God existing as an idea within the mind of believers rather than an external, objective being.

Following the series and the publication of the book, *The Sea of Faith* Society was formed, promoting this new understanding of religious faith. Religion needed to be believed and practised in new ways (see the section on postmodernism, below).

> **Sea of Faith** – a phrase taken from Matthew Arnold's poem 'Dover Beach', in which the poet likens the ebbing tide to the slipping away of belief in a supernatural world.

> **Key quote**
>
> 'God is the sum of our values, representing to us their ideal unity, their claims upon us and their creative power.'
>
> (Don Cupitt)

Now test yourself

Tested ☐

1 Explain why the following were reasons for the rise of atheism: (a) objections to moral absolutes, (b) awareness of other faiths.

2 Explain what is meant by the phrase 'God is dead'.

Answers online

The nature of atheism

Positive atheism

Revised ☐

Positive atheism is the claim that no God or gods exist. It is also sometimes referred to as 'strong atheism'. Positive atheism asserts that you know that God does not exist. This might be because you think there is a lack of proof of the existence of God, or that belief in God is logically absurd or the idea is meaningless.

The term 'positive atheism' appears to have been first used in this sense by the philosopher Antony Flew at least as early as 1976 and has become common in philosophical, scholarly writing on atheism and theism.

Negative atheism

Revised ☐

Negative atheism is the lack of a positive belief in God or gods without an assertion that God or gods do not exist. It is also sometimes referred to as 'weak atheism'. Negative atheism can include children and adults who have never heard of God. It can also include people who have heard of God but have never given the idea of God any considerable thought.

Distinction from agnosticism

The term 'agnostic' was first used by the English biologist Thomas Huxley in a speech at a meeting of the Metaphysical Society in 1869. The word is derived from the Greek, meaning 'without knowledge'. Agnosticism embraces the idea that the existence of God or any ultimate reality is, in principle, unknowable. Our knowledge is limited, and we cannot know ultimate reasons for things. It is not that the evidence is lacking, it is that the evidence is never possible.

Some use the word differently. Agnosticism is commonly used to indicate a suspension of the decision to accept or reject belief in God – the suspension lasts until we have more data. In the last few years, for some, the meaning has shifted yet again. The philosopher Nicholas Everitt, in *The Non-existence of God* (2004), uses it to apply to someone who thinks God's existence and his non-existence are equally probable. This usage reflects the **postmodern** (see below) idea of rejecting absolute certainties about knowledge.

Agnosticism rejects the strong atheist position, since the strong atheist asserts there is no God. Agnosticism is more akin to weak atheism. Neither claims that God does not exist, and neither claims that God does exist. A weak atheist says that it might be possible to know for certain that God does not exist. The agnostic says that it is not possible to know.

> **Postmodern** – in philosophy, this refers to the period in Western history from the late twentieth century, characterised by broad scepticism, subjectivism and a general suspicion of reason.

Now test yourself

Tested ☐

3 Explain the differences between (a) positive and negative atheism, (b) negative atheism and agnosticism.

Answer online

> **Exam tip**
>
> Make sure that when you are answering a question on atheism you explain each key term that you use. A way to do this is by selecting the appropriate examples and evidence.

Responses to the challenge of atheism

One religious response is to ignore the challenges. God is seen as the only true source of knowledge. If there is a challenge, then the challenge must be in error.

Another approach is to accept the challenges as having validity and adapt the beliefs and practices of religion accordingly. This is similar to the postmodernist view of religion (see the section below).

A third approach is to address the challenges directly.

Challenges and possible responses

Revised ☐

The table highlights the challenges and possible responses.

Challenge of atheism	Religious responses
Science	The theories of the **Big Bang** and evolution (see Chapter 4.2) do not necessarily deny the existence of God.
	For many religious believers, the more they understand the workings of the universe, the more they see evidence of God.
	Science is trying to answer the 'how' questions whereas religion is trying to answer the 'why' questions.
	Science is based totally on human observation and reason. Religion is based partly on divine revelation.
	Science tends to be impersonal but religion tends to be concerned with the personal.

> **Big Bang theory** – the theory of an expanding universe that began as infinitely dense energy at some finite time in the past; the initial explosion that caused it to expand is called the Big Bang.

Empiricism	The cosmological and design arguments for the existence of God (see Chapters 3.1 and 4.3) appeal to empirical evidence to argue for a creator and designer.
	There are limits to empirical evidence. Sense experience cannot account for all human beliefs.
Evil and suffering	**Theodicies** provide possible justifications for God allowing evil and suffering (for example, God foresaw the fall of human beings and planned their **redemption** through Christ; the presence of evil helps people to grow and develop; a genuinely free person must be allowed to harm themselves and others).
	Some actions cause evil and suffering. However, we need to know what consequences our actions have if we are to make rational choices. Therefore, we must be allowed to act in a way that may cause evil and suffering.
Objection to moral absolutes	Where does moral obligation come from in a secular society and to whom are we obligated?
	Situation Ethics (see Chapter 1.2) argues that no act can always be right or wrong, it depends on the situation. However, its basis is the moral absolute 'Love your neighbour'.
	The rejection of moral absolutes was more the result of atheism than the cause of atheism.
Awareness of other faiths	Not all religions are true, but one or more might be.
	The variety of religions may be different routes to the same mountain top and so all are equally valid.

Redemption – to be brought back. In Christian terms, to be delivered from sin.

Theodicy – a justification of the righteousness of God, given the existence of evil.

Situation Ethics – a theory of ethics according to which moral rules are not absolutely binding but may be modified in the light of specific situations.

Now test yourself

4 Explain two possible responses to the challenge of atheism posed by empiricism.

5 What is meant by a 'theodicy'? Give an example of a theodicy.

Answers online

Tested ☐

Postmodernism

Key ideas in the postmodernist view of religion

Revised ☐

The period in which we now live is often called 'postmodern'. Postmodernism is composed of two parts – 'post' meaning 'after' and 'modernism' referring to the **modern** period. In philosophy, the start of the modern period is usually dated from Descartes (1596–1650). Descartes believed in exact science and objective knowledge. He was a **rationalist**. Postmodernism rejects the idea of objective knowledge.

Postmodernism has also rejected the idea of a **grand narrative**. In the Middle Ages, belief in God and the Bible gave society a grand narrative in which an all-powerful and all-loving God created and sustained the world. In the modernist period, knowledge and information were important. Truth could be discovered through reason and experience. A key idea of postmodernism is the rejection of any grand narrative. Knowledge is seen as dependent on a person's perspective; therefore, truth is seen as relative rather than absolute.

Religions as cultural constructs

A postmodernist view is that there is no objective knowledge or absolute representation of reality. Our concepts and the way we categorise and see the world are formed and influenced by the particular culture or society we live in. Religion is also seen as a **cultural construct**. Religion reflects the way society expects people to behave. Religions need to be deconstructed and then it will be seen that religious claims have no claim to absolute truth but are merely relative and subjective.

Modern – in philosophy, this refers to the period in Western history from about the time of the scientific revolution of the sixteenth and seventeenth centuries to the mid-twentieth century.

Rationalist – someone who believes the primary basis for knowledge is reason rather than experience.

Grand narrative – sometimes referred to as a meta-narrative. In this usage, a narrative is a history or story that is regarded as a true account of reality.

Cultural construct – the view that the characteristics people attribute to such social categories as race or status of women are defined by the culture. They are arbitrary and can change.

Exam practice answers at **www.therevisionbutton.co.uk/myrevisionnotes**

No right or wrong religions

Because they are seen as cultural constructs, religions can make no claim to be true. There can be no 'right' or 'wrong' religions. They all merely reflect their culture. Therefore, people can choose which religion, if any, is most suitable for them. There is no judgement as all values and religious ideas are acceptable. Being truly religious is not about following specific **dogmas** or certainties but of truly loving God.

Personal spiritual search

Postmodernism does not hold to the idea of 'One True Religion' and remains agnostic about whether God exists and what 'God' means. Therefore, the emphasis is on individual choice – the personal spiritual search.

The religious supermarket and the pick and mix approach

The view that there are no right or wrong religions and the emphasis on a personal spiritual search allow the individual to select their own narrative. This could be from traditional religions or from less traditional religions. The narrative can even be a combination from several different religions, known as a pick and mix approach.

Living religion rather than intellectual faith

Because religions are seen as cultural constructs which make no claim to be true, the emphasis has centred on religion as a way of life rather than a system of beliefs. Therefore, religion cannot be based on intellectual faith.

Now test yourself

Tested

6   What is meant by the phrase 'religion is a cultural construct'?

Answer online

Issues arising

Is religion in retreat in the modern world?

Revised

One of the major issues arising is whether religion is in retreat in the modern world.

To support 'in retreat'	To challenge 'in retreat'
Evidence of secularisation, e.g. decline in the authority of religious institutions and rejection of moral absolutes.	Growth of religions worldwide (sects and mainstream faiths).
Evidence of rejection of traditional religion – both in belief and attendance.	Growth in spirituality and postmodern living-faith without assenting to a particular set of beliefs.
Evidence of rejection of dogmas and certainty.	Lack of certainty in science.

Dogma – prescribed doctrine proclaimed as unquestionably true by the Church.

Key quote
'Facts are precisely what there is not, only interpretations.'
(Friedrich Nietzsche)

Key quote
'At the modern supermarket of faith, the consumer seeks to pick and mix religious items to match their commitment and faith.'
(James Beckford, British sociologist)

Key quote
'Religious truth, being truly religious, is not a formula to recite but a deed to do … The name of God is something to do.'
(John Caputo, American philosopher)

Exam tip
Do not use quotations just to repeat what you have written. You need either to explain how the quote illustrates your point or to draw out some further comment from the quote.

Typical mistake
It is a mistake to list criticisms in the style of a shopping list, since no evaluation is being demonstrated. The skill of evaluation involves demonstrating a process of reasoning. This means giving arguments to defend a view and using analysis to critique those arguments so that the conclusion reached is justified.

Is postmodernism an affirmation of religion?

Postmodernism *is* an affirmation of religion	Postmodernism is *not* an affirmation of religion
Allows religion to be seen in a wider context – freed from dogma and particular statements of belief. It allows a religious interpretation of life that otherwise might have been rejected because it was not intellectually justifiable.	Denies intellectual knowledge of God.
	Is more agnosticism than religion.
	Allows any belief and therefore has no content.
Is concerned with spiritual living – the heart of religion – not intellectual knowledge of God.	Denies ultimate truth whereas traditional religions claim revelation and ultimate truths.
Puts the importance on practical actions – the outworking of religious faith.	Is really atheism since it can have an anti-realist view of God, i.e. it rejects the objective existence of a supernatural being (God).
Interprets traditional religion for the postmodern era.	Treats believers as consumers (pick and mix approach) – religion is not something that can be bought or rejected on the basis of what you like or prefer.
Widens the meaning of both religion and God.	

How successfully has religion responded to the challenge of atheism?

This requires a weighing-up of the success, or failure, of the arguments and responses listed in the table on pages 108–109. Ask yourself some key questions about the responses to the challenge of atheism:

- How much of a threat to religion is the Darwinian theory of evolution (see Chapter 4.2)?
- Does religion only answer 'why' questions and never a 'how' question?
- To what extent are the cosmological and design arguments (see Chapters 3.1 and 4.3) successful in arguing for the existence of God?
- Does religion successfully address the problem of **natural evil**?
- Is morality not possible without God?
- Are all religions equally valid?

> **Natural evil** – events which cause suffering but over which human beings have little or no control, such as earthquakes and diseases.

Now test yourself
Tested ☐

7 How would you respond to the argument that secularisation shows that religion is in retreat in the modern world?

8 Explain why the argument that 'all religions are equally valid' can be used to support both atheism and religion.

Answers online

> **Typical mistake**
>
> Make sure you leave enough time to answer the 15-mark question. Some candidates run out of time and so give very limited answers that gain few marks.

Exam practice

(a) Explain the key ideas of a postmodernist view of religion. (30 marks)

(b) To what extent is postmodernism a denial of religion rather than an affirmation? (15 marks)

Answers online

Online ☐

4.1 Miracles

A miracle as a violation of Natural Law

Hume's definition of 'miracle'
Revised

The understanding of a miracle as a violation of Natural Law involves some intervention by God, without which the event would not have taken place. The intervention is usually seen in terms of the breaking of a **law of nature**. David Hume, an eighteenth-century Scottish philosopher, defined miracles as: 'a transgression (violation) of a law of nature by a particular volition of the Deity or by the interposition of some invisible agent.'

> **Law of nature** – a generalisation based on regular happenings within nature, such as the law of gravity.

A miracle occurs when the world is not left to itself, when something distinct from the natural order as a whole intrudes into it, such as God. Examples include:

- the healing of a man with a withered arm, restoring the limb to its normal state
- raising from the dead to full health someone whose heart had stopped for over 24 hours and who by modern criteria was classed as brain-dead
- walking on water with no support under the water and without the feet sinking into the water.

Implications for religious understandings of the way God interacts with the world
Revised

This view that miracles are a breaking of a law of nature could be seen as putting God into the role of spectator of events. He is a God who is outside of the universe and who observes events. At times he enters our world to change events by suspending natural laws. Religious believers may argue that prayer is consistent with such a view, in that, in praying, believers are asking God to intervene.

Some also combine a belief that miracles break laws of nature with a belief that laws of nature are the means by which God sustains the universe.

Challenges to the idea of an interventionist God
Revised

1 An interventionist God moves in, but only occasionally. This is contrary to **classical theism**, where God is seen as sustainer and preserver of the universe and the world is dependent on God's sustaining activity for its existence.
2 An interventionist God would have to be limited to the time frame of the event in order to intervene. This is incompatible with the idea of God being outside of time.

> **Classical theism** – the belief in a personal deity, creator of everything that exists, who is distinct from that creation and is sustainer and preserver of the universe.

3 If God is able to intervene, then why doesn't he address the real problems of the world more directly by means of miracles? This is part of the problem of evil and suffering. God has the means (power) and the motivation (love, goodness) to eliminate evil and suffering. Yet there is evil and suffering. God seems indifferent to the continued existence of suffering in the world.

A recent professor of divinity at Oxford University, Maurice Wiles, argued that a God who acts in such a trivial way is a God not worthy of worship. This implies that miracles do not happen if belief in a traditional God is to be maintained.

Exam tip

Remember to explain fully each point that you make in an exam answer. Think carefully about each sentence and how it relates to the question and the previous sentence.

Hume's arguments against violations of Natural Law and exceptions

Revised

According to Hume, the argument of miracles could never be used to demonstrate the truth of Christianity or religion in general. His case rests on the view that the evidence from past testimony of miracles could never outweigh our present-day experience of the regularity of nature. He argues the following points:

- A wise man proportions his belief to the evidence.
- A miracle is a violation of the laws of nature.
- Laws of nature have been established by a uniform experience over a period of many hundreds of years.
- It is more reasonable to believe that the law of nature has held and not been broken, than to believe testimony claiming that the law of nature has been broken *unless* the testimony be of such a kind that its falsehood would be more miraculous than the fact which it endeavours to establish.

Hume's distrust of testimonies of past miracles

Revised

Hume then highlighted several reasons why testimony can never be of that calibre and therefore it is more rational to distrust the testimony about a miracle than to believe that the law of nature has been broken. His distrust of all such testimony of past miracles was because:

- No miracle had a sufficient number of witnesses (what is required is a quantity of educated trustworthy witnesses to a public event – people who would have a lot to lose if found to be lying).
- People are prone to look for marvels and wonders.
- The source of miracle stories are from ignorant people – miracle stories acquire authority without critical or rational inquiry.
- The writers had a vested interest and so there was bias – this was especially true if a miracle was being used to establish a religion (e.g. the Resurrection).
- Religious traditions counteract each other – this argument is different from the others in that unreliability here does not derive from the unreliability of the witnesses; rather that the evidence is further contradicted by other witnesses (for example, Muhammad's ascension into heaven supports Islam and so discredits Christianity as a true.

Typical mistake

Candidates often begin their accounts of Hume's arguments with a lengthy paragraph recounting irrelevant biographical details. Marks are awarded for the demonstration of an understanding of the arguments, not for potted biographies.

religion, so any claim of Christian miracle, such as Jesus' resurrection from the dead, will discredit Islam).

Hume concludes that it is therefore never reasonable to believe in miracles. The testimony will always be weaker than the evidence for uniform laws of nature.

Now test yourself   Tested

1 State Hume's definition of a miracle.
2 State the five reasons that Hume gave as to why testimony of past miracles could not be trusted.

Answers online

Scientific arguments which challenge Hume's definition of a miracle

Revised

- Our understanding of the laws of nature is flawed. If laws of nature are generalisations formulated retrospectively to cover what has happened, then there cannot be miracles. For whenever any event happens that is outside of the established natural laws, it would simply mean that we must widen the law to cover this new case. In this understanding, supposed laws of nature are not broken but are better described as incomplete laws that now have to be adapted to include the new happening.

- The new view of the universe is not necessarily mechanistic and predictable. Quantum physics suggests that nature displays **indeterminism** and unpredictability. Therefore, it may no longer be necessary to insist that God must 'suspend' or 'violate' natural laws in order to directly act in our world.

- Laws of nature merely describe what we expect to happen given certain conditions. When these conditions are changed then the 'law' does not apply. When a miracle occurs, the initial conditions are different, since God's special activity is now a new, added condition. Hence the 'law' has not been broken.

- To conclude that an event is caused by God because it appears to break a law of nature is to resort to a **'God of the gaps'** argument. Science may have some unanswered questions – things that, as yet, have not been explained. However, it does not justify religious believers to argue that if science cannot explain how something happened, then God must be the explanation. Such arguments are called 'God of the gaps' arguments.

Key quote

'"We may be mistaken" is a knife which cuts both ways – we may be mistaken in believing that an event is not a divine intervention when really it is, as well as the other way around.'

(Richard Swinburne)

Indeterminism – the theory that states that not every event has a cause.

God of the gaps – gaps in scientific knowledge are taken to be evidence or proof of God's existence.

General responses to arguments

Arguments against and in support of Hume's definition of 'miracle'

Arguments against Hume's definition	Responses which support Hume's definition
Classical theism views God as sustainer not observer.	God as sustainer does not deny the possibility that God also intervenes.
God would be limited in time.	It is not clear what 'outside of time' or 'limited by time' actually mean. Whatever they do mean, why is it assumed that God cannot be both outside and inside of time?
Trivial acts.	Theodicies attempt to address the problem of evil.
	God acts to accomplish his purpose for the universe. Part of that purpose is to reveal himself and make himself known.
	If there are other reasons for believing that God is loving, then God may have reasons for these apparently trivial acts that we do not fully understand.
There has never been any event that has broken the laws of nature.	Hume's argument that no miracle has had a sufficient number of witnesses is a big assumption (e.g. the resurrection of Jesus was witnessed by up to 500 according to Paul; Angels of Mons were witnessed by hundreds).
	Testimony is not the only evidence for miracles. For example, physical effects can be seen such as a healed withered arm; X-rays can provide evidence of a 'before' and 'after' situation.
	When comparing one miracle with another, it is important to note that the evidence may be much weightier for one miracle than for another.
Hume's definition contradicts known science.	Science is not invalidated. If God intervenes and 'from time to time breaks the laws of nature' then it only follows that science's predictions based on those laws will be incorrect 'from time to time'.
	Science has limitations.
	There is no entity called 'science' that can authoritatively rule whether miracles can or cannot happen. Science is neutral.
	It is rational to believe that a miracle has occurred, while allowing the possibility that evidence might turn up later to show that we are mistaken.
Events that appear to break laws of nature have a natural explanation. There is no need for recourse to a 'God of the gaps' argument.	To claim that no event ever breaks a law of nature is to go against the scientific method. Science cannot rule whether laws of nature can or cannot be broken.

Exam tip

Always refer back to the focus of the question in your answers by picking up the focus of the question in the first sentence of each of your paragraphs. This will make sure that you do not move away from the focus and so will avoid you drifting into irrelevant material.

Theodicies – justifications of the righteousness of God, given the existence of evil.

Now test yourself

3   Explain the following response to the scientific challenge against miracles: 'There is no entity called "science" that can authoritatively rule whether miracles can or cannot happen.'

Answer online

A miracle as an event of religious significance

The philosopher Richard Swinburne (b. 1934) agreed that miracles were examples of the breaking of the laws of nature but argued that miracles also needed to hold some deeper significance than just this. He claimed that miracles were objective events. If God had not intervened, the event would not have occurred. Swinburne also regarded Hume's description of 'violations of laws of nature' as misleading and instead favoured the phrase 'counter instances to a law of nature'.

The concept of a miracle as an event of religious significance may refer to a number of different types of events.

Signs

The Judeo-Christian tradition, by which miracles are seen as signs from God, gives support to this understanding. The miracles point to something beyond the actual event and are not seen as an end in themselves. The word 'sign' is used in John's Gospel to refer to Jesus' miracles. In this view, Hume's definition needs refining to fully capture the meaning of 'miracle'. While not denying that God intervenes in a supernatural way, the focus is about the religious significance of the intervention; i.e. what God is disclosing.

An example of this is the phenomenon of stigmata. Stigmata are bodily marks, sores or sensations of pain in parts of the body corresponding to the crucifixion wounds of Jesus, such as the hands and feet. Often they are accompanied by a vision or some other religious experience. The first recorded stigmatic in Christian history is St Francis of Assisi, whose stigma appeared after a vision of a seraph who was suffering and attached to a cross.

Other philosophers have focused solely on the religious significance aspect and denied the supernatural intervention. This is an interpretative view of miracles that interprets natural events as having religious significance.

Amazing coincidences and natural events

It is the religious interpretation that makes it a miracle. Only if a person interprets the event as a miracle can the event be called a miracle. No law of nature is broken. This contrasts with the view that if God intervenes to break the law of nature, then it is a miracle regardless of whether anyone recognises it or not. However, some religious believers may agree with both definitions of miracles, seeing God sometimes working in a more spectacular way by breaking a law of nature, and at other times seemingly acting through natural events.

A famous illustration of the amazing coincidence type of event was given by Ray Holland, an American philosopher. Holland claimed that an event that has an explanation within natural laws can be considered a miracle, if it is taken religiously as a sign. He called these 'contingency miracles'. He used an illustration to explain this understanding of miracles. Holland tells of a child riding a toy car, caught between the rail tracks with a train fast approaching out of sight of the boy. The mother could see both the boy on the track and the train approaching. She realised the train could not stop in time once the driver saw the boy. However, the train suddenly started to slow down before the boy came into view and came to a halt a metre away from the boy, leaving him unharmed. The mother thanked God and saw it as a miracle, even when she learnt that the train stopped because the driver suffered a heart condition and the automatic braking system came into play.

Now test yourself

Tested

4   Explain how Swinburne's understanding of miracles differs from Ray Holland's understanding of miracles.

Answer online

Exam tip

It is important to explain how the story of the boy on the train tracks illustrates the definition of a miracle. Allude to the story rather than spend a page graphically retelling it.

Key quote

'If a god intervened in the natural order to make a feather land here rather than there for no deep ultimate purpose, or to upset a child's box of toys just for spite, these events would not naturally be described as miracles.'

(Richard Swinburne)

Implications of an interpretative view of miracles for the way God interacts with the world

- This understanding of miracles does not see God as an interventionist but as a sustainer of the world. The world is dependent on God's sustaining activity for its existence but does not involve God in specific actions.

- God can providentially order the world so that natural causes of events are ready and waiting to produce certain other events at the right time, perhaps in answer to prayers which God knew would be offered.

- God transforms us and we transform the world. So God transforms the world through us.

- Quantum physics suggests that nature sometimes displays indeterminism. It is no longer necessary to insist that God must 'suspend' or 'violate' natural laws in order to act directly.

Religious response to an interpretative view of miracles

- The reason why many people believe in God at all is because they are persuaded that he has intervened supernaturally in an historical event (for example, the resurrection of Jesus).

- In many religions their sacred writings are recordings of supernatural events to vindicate the claims of those who are accepted as God's messengers on Earth.

- Sacred writings not only contain a vast number of descriptions of apparent supernatural events but also give virtually no hint that these events are intended to be interpreted figuratively rather than literally. Even the use of the word 'sign' in John's Gospel does not indicate that the events did not literally happen. Events can be both symbolic and literal.

Now test yourself

5. Explain why an interpretative view of miracles implies a different view of the way God interacts with the world, to that of an interventionist view of miracles.

6. State two reasons based on the contents of sacred writings that challenge the interpretative view of miracles.

Answers online

Key quote

'Nothing is esteemed a miracle, if it ever happens in the common course of nature.'

(David Hume)

Issues arising

The strengths and weaknesses of the arguments from David Hume and from science

Revised

This requires you to weigh up how strong or weak the various arguments are. The various arguments and responses can be found above on pages 111–118. It means discussing how persuasive they are, rather than just stating what the arguments are.

For instance, consider the challenge to belief in miracles based on the argument that the testimony of a miracle can never outweigh the belief that the law of nature has been broken. Hume cites a number of reasons, including the absence of sufficient numbers of quality witnesses. It could be argued that Hume's argument is reasonable since the witnesses must be trustworthy and reliable. However, a weakness in the argument may be that it is not clear how many witnesses are required to qualify for 'sufficient'. Is belief ultimately based on the number of witnesses? Maybe the nature of the event and the extent it is consistent with the nature of God and his purposes is more significant than how many witnesses there are to the event.

Hume seems to write as if all believers were either deceivers or the deceived. In his chapter on miracles in his book *Enquiry Concerning Human Understanding*, he cited some miracles that occurred in France and which supposedly took place in his own lifetime. Hume acknowledged that the events were witnessed by people of unquestioned integrity. However, Hume refused to credit such testimony on the grounds of 'the absolute impossibility or miraculous nature of the events which they relate'. This implies that Hume rejected miracles regardless of the evidence. However, as an empiricist he surely should go by the evidence. It raises the wider question as to the extent that weight of evidence can persuade us to change our minds.

Remember that weighing up involves evaluation and not just reciting the arguments.

If miracles happen, do they make it reasonable to believe that God exists?

Revised

The most important aspect in this issue is to clearly identify which definition of miracle you are discussing. This means taking each definition in turn and discussing the claim as to whether it is reasonable to believe in the light of the miracle happening.

It is important to note that the claim assumes the miracle has taken place. Therefore, no marks would be credited for discussion about whether the miracle did or did not happen.

The concept of 'reasonable' also needs discussion. For something to be reasonable implies that the argument and lines of reasoning are capable of moving an unprejudiced person to accept the conclusion as persuasive. The conclusion based on the reasoning is more likely to be true than false. However, it does not guarantee the conclusion is true.

The table on the next page gives some pointers about the two definitions of miracles and whether they lead to belief in God.

Now test yourself

7 What are the strengths and weaknesses of the argument that Hume's definition of 'miracle' cannot be true because God does not seem to intervene to deal with the world's real problems?

Answer online

Tested

Exam tip

Do not feel that you must always reach a conclusion. Not being able to reach a conclusion is an acceptable answer. However, there has to be justification in your answer as to why no one particular conclusion can be fully supported. The AO2 descriptor is 'justify a point of view through the use of evidence and reasoned argument'.

Definition of miracle	Leads to belief in God	Does *not* lead to belief in God
Breaking of law of nature.	Clear evidence of God – no other reasonable explanation.	Alternative explanations, e.g. naturalistic, some other supernatural being.
	Consistent with God's nature and purposes, e.g. wanting to make himself known.	The trivial and infrequent interventions suggest a monster God. Not a loving God of classical theism.
	Consistent with events in sacred texts.	Sacred texts contain mythological language. Not accounts of literal events.
		Sacred texts are stories of people's search for something beyond themselves. They are not from God.
Religious significance/ interpretation.	Consistent with our understanding of the way God works in the universe, i.e. God working through evolution and free will choices.	We have no idea how a God would work in the universe.
	People worldwide experience this guidance/disclosure from God and it changes their lives.	All events can be explained without recourse to a God.
		Psychological/coincidence explanation.

If God exists, would God intervene to perform a miracle if asked?

Revised

Note that the issue assumes there is a God, so no credit would be awarded for discussion that miracles do not happen because there is no God.

This issue requires discussion about the following:

- **The definition of miracle that is being discussed:** miracles seen as interpretations of events pose difficulties in terms of the idea of asking God to intervene. The only way to argue would be that God can providentially order the world so that natural causes of such events are ready and waiting at the right time, thus providing an answer to prayer which God knew would be offered.

- **The circumstances in which God may or may not act:** again, this would depend on what is being asked for and why. It may also depend on who is doing the asking. For instance, would God be more likely to respond to a believer than an unbeliever?

- **What it is that God is being asked to do:** the miracle would have to be consistent with God's nature and purposes. Asking for selfish things that would diminish our spiritual growth would seem unlikely to be granted. Even things that we might regard as beneficial may not be consistent with God's ultimate purposes. We can only see things from a human and earthly dimension.

- **Whether miracles are things God can ever be persuaded to do:** ultimately, God is sovereign and in control. His purposes cannot be thwarted. However, some religious sacred texts indicate that God answers prayer, including persistent prayer.

Exam practice

(a) Explain the difficulties raised for religious believers by defining a miracle as 'an amazing coincidence of religious significance'. **(30 marks)**

(b) Assess the extent to which defining a miracle as 'violation of a law by a supernatural agent' overcomes these difficulties. **(15 marks)**

Answers online

Online

Now test yourself

8 Give two arguments to support the view that miracles that are defined as interpretations do not lead to a belief in God.

Answer online

Tested

4.2 Creation

Religious beliefs about the creation of the world

Most religious beliefs about creation can be found in written accounts. These can be interpreted in different ways:

- **Creationists** interpret written accounts literally. Among creationists there is a debate about the extent to which the accounts are literally true.

- Non-creationists consider the written accounts to be full of meaning but the words used are not usually to be understood literally.

> **Creationist** – a person who believes that humanity, life and the universe are the creation of a supernatural being. Creationists can be 'Young Earth' or 'Old Earth' creationists.

Literal interpretation of the creation story

Revised

Young Earth creationism ('six-day')

This is a term that describes the belief that the universe and life were created by God over a very short period. It suggests a sudden and complete process rather than one that stretches over millions of years. It is usually associated with a very literal interpretation of religious texts, such as the creation account in the early chapters of Genesis in the Old Testament. This account depicts God creating the universe (and life) in eight divine acts over a period of six days:

- Let there be light … (Genesis 1:3)
- Let there be an expanse between the waters … (Genesis 1:6)
- Let the water under the sky be gathered together … (Genesis1:9)
- Let the land produce vegetation … (Genesis 1:11)
- Let there be lights in the expanse of the sky … (Genesis 1:14)
- Let the water teem with living creatures, and let birds fly … (Genesis 1:20)
- Let the land produce living creatures … (Genesis 1:24)
- Let us make man in our image … (Genesis 1:26)

This literal approach to the Genesis account sees the seven days as 24-hour days during which God created the world. The characteristics of each species, including human beings, were fully developed at the time of creation.

> **Exam tip**
>
> When discussing religious beliefs about creation, do not assume that all religious believers have the same viewpoint, or that they refer to the same source of authority.

Old Earth creationism

There are various forms of this position, listed below. (The list is not exhaustive.)

1 **Progressive creationism (day-age theory)**

This view proposes that each day of the creation week in Genesis represents a long age in which God acted upon creation. In other

> **Key quote**
>
> 'Buddhism and science share a fundamental reluctance to postulate a transcendent being as the origin of all things.'
>
> (The Dalai Lama)

words, the word 'day' is not taken literally as 'a 24-hour period', but is understood to mean simply 'a period of time'. Therefore, it would fit in with the view that the Earth is billions of years old. This view would accept adaptation within a species, but might argue that human beings are special creations and not evolved from another species.

2 **Gap theory**

Many argue that a gap should be inserted between Genesis 1:1 and Genesis 1:2. This then accommodates geological time and allows for an Earth that is billions of years old.

3 **God as the source of the Big Bang**

The **Big Bang theory** is seen as consistent with the claim that there is a God. Both the Big Bang theory and Genesis say that the universe had a beginning and that both time and space came from nothing. God is seen as the explanation of the Big Bang. In 1951, Pope Pius XII declared approval for the Big Bang based on this understanding. Similarly, evolution can be seen as God's chosen mechanism through which human beings came into existence.

4 **The theory of intelligent design**

This theory argues that intelligence is necessary to explain the complex, information-rich structures of biology and that this intelligence is **empirically** detectable. The major evidence is based on **irreducible complexities**. This means that all parts of a system must be in place at the same time for the system to work. The different parts could not have arisen separately, or at different times, by a process of gradual change such as **natural selection**. The conclusion that there needs to be an intelligent designer implies that God is the designer.

> **Big Bang theory** – the theory of an expanding universe that began as infinitely dense energy at some finite time in the past; the initial explosion that caused it to expand is called the Big Bang.
>
> **Empirical** – relying on or derived from observation or experiment.
>
> **Irreducible complexities** – intelligent design argues that certain biological systems are too complex to have evolved through natural selection. These complex systems only function when all parts are together but each of the parts has no independent function.
>
> **Natural selection** – a key mechanism of evolution. It is the principle by which each slight variation, if useful, is preserved and the trait passed on to the next generation.

Non-creationist interpretation of the creation story

Revised

A religious non-creationist understanding of the creation stories believes them to be important for the meaning they contain. Sometimes the word 'myth' is used to describe the accounts. Myths are symbolic narratives that show how people relate to both the spiritual and natural world as well as to each other. They convey profound truths but not in a historical or literal sense. They are more about questions of meaning and purpose – the 'why' questions, rather than the 'how' questions that science focuses on.

In 1964, Philip Freund wrote a book entitled *Myths of Creation*. In it he identified five types of myth:

1 **Water myths** see the cosmos as arising from some kind of misty, watery substance. The writer of Genesis depicts order emerging from the primeval waters of chaos.

2 In **egg myths** the 'birth' of the cosmos erupted from a basic physical formation and is seen as being directly related to the divine being.

3 **Dismemberment myths** involve a primordial monster or creature of some kind used to carve out creation.

4 **Mating of the gods myths** are where deities produce lesser deities that eventually give birth to the cosmos and human life.

5 The **edict myths** are where the spoken word or divine utterance caused the cosmos to come into existence.

> **Exam tip**
>
> Make sure that in the exam you use technical information correctly. Do not confuse key terms.

Some religious believers read the Genesis account as a myth that conveys truths about the nature of God. There is no attempt to try to link it to scientific theories. The truths include the following:

- Creation is distinct from God but dependent on God. The creator is separate and distinct from that which he creates.
- Creation is very good. The material creation is seen as good. The repetition of God's approval of his creation throughout the narrative in Genesis 1 ('and he saw that it was good') indicates the moral worth of creation. It gives creation a special, holy status.
- Creation is purposeful and ordered. God freely chose to create.
- God has authority over the creation. The creation does not belong to human beings. We hold the world in trust for God. The creation of Adam and Eve in the Garden of Eden shows that human beings have great responsibility within creation.
- God is all powerful. God only needs to speak words and creation comes into being.
- God is all knowing.

Exam tip

Be careful when using quotes. Always make sure that they are relevant by explaining how they relate to the point you are discussing.

Now test yourself

1 Explain how the Genesis account of creation can be seen as (a) contradicting science, (b) consistent with science.
2 'Myths are not true.' Give an argument to support this claim and give an argument that challenges this claim.

Answers online

Tested

God and the created world

God as sustainer
Revised

Many theists argue that it is important to understand that God is a sustaining God, because without this, he would be relegated to a divine starter and nothing more. Such a view would, in effect, characterise God as **deistic** rather than theistic. Therefore, creatures are totally dependent on God and would not survive without his conserving action. Religious views differ about the exact nature of God's sustaining actions. Some argue that the finely tuned balances in nature are evidence of a providential God. Others argue that religious experiences demonstrate God's sustaining interest in creation. Yet others argue that God works through the processes of nature – such as the Big Bang and evolution – guiding them ultimately to some divine end purpose.

Deistic – the belief in a God who created the universe and then exerts no influence on natural phenomena and gives no supernatural revelation.

The idea of God as sustainer is consistent with the idea of an interventionist God. However, some argue that it does not necessarily conflict with the idea of a non-interventionist God. Such a God could have providentially ordered the world so that natural causes of events are ready and waiting to produce certain other events at the right time, perhaps in answer to prayers which God knew would be offered.

Key ideas of deism
Revised

Deism became prominent in the seventeenth and eighteenth century during the **Enlightenment**. Its key ideas include the following:

- The universe was created by an all-powerful God.
- God does not intervene in human affairs.

Enlightenment – a philosophical movement of the eighteenth century that emphasised the use of reason.

- God does not suspend the laws of nature.
- God does not alter the universe by intervening in it. He allows it to run according to the laws of nature that he formed when he created all things.
- God is wholly **transcendent** and never **immanent**.
- God can only be known via reason and the observation of nature.

Transcendent – wholly independent of (and removed from) the material universe.

Immanent – fully present in the physical world and accessible to creatures in various ways.

Now test yourself   Tested ☐

3   What is meant by saying 'God is sustainer'?

4   Explain why deists think God can only be known through reason or through the observation of nature.

Answers online

Typical mistake

Candidates often make the mistake of recounting in detail a creation story (usually from Genesis) just because the word 'creation' appears in the exam question. Each question set will have a particular focus and it is the focus that must be addressed.

Scientific theories about the nature, origin and end of the universe

Cosmology is the scientific study of the origin and nature of the universe. The universe is more than just our solar system; it includes every physical thing that exists. The most favoured view about the origin of the universe is called the Big Bang theory, which argues for an expanding universe.

The Big Bang theory   Revised ☐

The name 'Big Bang' is slightly misleading as it gives the impression that an explosion occurred that caused matter to move outwards from a single point. There was neither an explosion nor a 'bang', but an expansion.

The Big Bang can be compared to a balloon – not a balloon popping and releasing its contents, but more like a balloon being blown up and continually growing.

The theory

Scientists disagree about some of the exact details but a basic outline of the Big Bang theory might be summarised as follows:

- Some 13.7 billion years ago nothing existed – not even space itself.
- An infinitely small and infinitely dense ball of energy, called a space–time singularity, appeared.
- It did not appear in space; rather space began inside the singularity.
- Mathematicians have calculated that after 10^{-43} **seconds** of its initial appearance, the singularity started to expand. A temporary, very rapid period of expansion called inflation occurred. As the singularity expanded, it started to cool.
- Between 10^{-12} and 10^{-6} seconds, the fundamental particles (quarks) appeared.
- Between 1 and 10 seconds, electrons formed, followed by photons (light).

10^{-43} **seconds** – this means $1/10^{43}$ seconds.

- Between 300,000 and 500,000 years after the initial appearance of the singularity, atoms formed. This is usually regarded as marking the end of the Big Bang.
- After about 100 million years, as the cooling continued, galaxies and stars started to be formed.
- The origin of the solar system can be traced to about nine thousand million years ago.

The evidence for the Big Bang

- Galaxies appear to be moving away from us at speeds proportional to their distance from us. In 1929, Edwin Hubble noticed that galactic light is slightly distorted in colour (known as 'red shift'). This suggests that every galaxy is moving away from every other one, which is consistent with the idea of an expanding universe.
- The theory is consistent with Albert Einstein's theories about gravity, in which he argued that gravity stretches or distorts space and time. Galaxies are moving further apart.
- The Big Bang theory suggests that initially the universe was extremely hot. In 1965, Arno Penzias and Robert Wilson discovered what they thought was some remnant of this heat (known as the 'cosmic microwave background radiation').
- The Big Bang creation model predicts the relative occurrence of hydrogen and helium in the universe. The predictions match what we actually find in the universe and so support the Big Bang creation model.

Key quote

'The universe has been expanding for billions of years, so there must have been a time in the ancient past when all the matter in the universe was concentrated in a state of infinite density.'

(William Kaufmann, professor of astrophysics)

Now test yourself

5 Why is the Big Bang theory an unsuitable name by which to describe it?

Answer online

Tested ☐

The 'Big Crunch'

Revised ☐

Just as the Big Bang describes how the universe most possibly began, the Big Crunch describes how it might end as a consequence of that beginning.

The theory

According to this theory, at a certain point in time, the universe will stop expanding. This will happen when the density of the universe is greater than what is called the 'critical density'. Then the strength of the gravitational force will stop the universe from expanding. As gravity pulls on the matter, the universe will begin to contract, falling inward until it has collapsed back into a super-hot, super-dense singularity.

Problems with the 'Big Crunch' theory

Previously, it was thought that the momentum of the Big Bang that pushes the galaxies out further would eventually be overcome by the gravitational force. However, recent tests suggest that the universe is continuing to expand. To explain this phenomenon, scientists have had to assume the presence of an unknown entity, which they call 'dark energy'. It is believed that this entity is pushing all galaxies farther apart.

As a result of the continuing expansion of the universe, it is generally thought that the Big Crunch is unlikely, and the universe will just carry on expanding. At present, cosmic expansion is actually accelerating.

Exam tip

Remember not to confuse assessment objectives. AO1 for 30 marks asks you to examine, explain or outline, but not to assess or evaluate. Therefore, if asked to explain how the universe most probably began, do not start discussing criticisms of the theories.

Endless expansion

Another theory argues that the universe did not begin with the Big Bang.

The theory

- The universe goes through an endless sequence of cycles in which it contracts into a Big Crunch and re-emerges in an expanding Big Bang.
- The Big Bang is the beginning of just one of a possibly infinite number of cycles.
- The transition from Big Crunch to Big Bang automatically replenishes the universe by creating new matter and radiation.

The evidence for the theory of endless expansion

- The theory is consistent with all the evidence that supports the Big Bang theory.
- It addresses the questions that the Big Bang was unable to address (e.g. What happened before the Big Bang?).
- Previously, this theory was rejected because the laws of physics showed that it was impossible. However, modern physics questions the view that the basic constituents of matter are particles. An alternative view is string theory. In this view, particles are replaced by a single fundamental building block, a 'string'. This would allow for an endless expansion of the universe.

The modern cosmological theories attempt to explain both the start and the end of the universe. Both these explanations have implications for religious belief.

The start of the universe

Those religious believers who see an Old Earth and a beginning to the universe do not necessarily regard the Big Bang as a challenge to religious belief. They see the modern scientific accounts of cosmology as consistent with the existence of a God. What they reject is the idea that the appearance of the singularity has a natural explanation. The religious believer sees that the explanation for the appearance of the singularity is God. Without God there would have been no universe. Religious believers respond by denying that the universe can be explained wholly by **materialism**. Also they deny that the scientific method is the only valid source of knowledge.

> **Materialism** – a theory that regards matter as the only reality in the universe.

Modern cosmologies also challenge religious belief by implying that the universe has no meaning or purpose. The universe is depicted as something coming about by chance rather than deliberate purpose. Religious believers may respond by arguing that science can only consider the means (the 'how' question) while religion also considers reasons (the 'why' question). Therefore science is unable to comment on issues of purpose and meaning.

Those religious believers who argue for a Young Earth, of necessity do not accept the findings of modern cosmology. They respond by arguing that the cosmological theories are flawed in some way. For instance, they raise doubts over the existence of 'dark energy'. For them, the religious

> **Exam tip**
>
> Explain each point that you make in your exam answer. Think carefully about each sentence and how it relates to the question and the previous sentence. Aim for at least three sentences to explain a point. For example, state what the point is, how it is understood, and then, if appropriate, give an example. This will help to ensure 'a thorough treatment of the topic within the time available.' (AO1)

text, seen as the word of God, is the source of truth rather than scientific theories that constantly change.

The end of the universe

Modern cosmologies offer a number of theories about the state of the cosmos in the far future. For example a universe that:

● goes on in time for ever

● continues to expand and, because of this expansion, it continues to cool down until it will be too cold to support any life

● eventually collapses back into a super-hot, super-dense singularity.

While the idea of the end of the world does not necessarily conflict with religion, this event is usually seen by religious believers as being caused by a direct intervention by God. This is in contrast to the scientific idea of the cause being in the very fabric of the universe. According to the religious believer, if the universe comes to an end then it will be because God has willed it so.

Key quote

'The intention of the Holy Ghost is to teach us how one goes to heaven, not how heaven goes.'

(Galileo)

Key quote

'… we certainly cannot use science to tell us what existed before the Big Bang. These things are fundamentally unknowable. The phrases "before the Big Bang" or "at the moment of the Big Bang" are meaningless, because time itself did not really exist.'

(William Kaufmann)

Now test yourself

Tested

6 Explain two problems with the 'Big Crunch' theory.

7 Explain a response to the challenge that the universe has a natural explanation and does not require the need of a God to explain its occurrence.

Answers online

Scientific theory about the origin and development of life

Evolutionary theory

Revised

Charles Darwin published his theory of evolution in 1859 (*On the Origin of Species*). His theory provided a way of understanding the natural world, in which its complex biological functions no longer required an intelligent designer to account for apparent order.

The theory

● Darwin identified that variations occur in offspring within a species. These are accidental.

● He proposed that organisms that are best able to survive (for example, by avoiding predators) pass on their genetic traits and so perpetuate these qualities to succeeding generations. This is known as natural selection.

● Darwin used the phrase 'survival of the fittest' but did not mean by it that only the fittest organisms would survive. He meant it to refer to those organisms that were better adapted for the immediate, local environment.

- The combination of variation and survival eventually leads to the emergence of organisms that are better suited to their environment.
- The particular variations that are favoured will effect a gradual transformation in the appearance and behaviour of the species.
- Over time, beneficial mutations accumulate and the result is an entirely different organism.
- Recent development of the theory has centred on the mechanisms of evolution, in particular the genetic changes that alter embryonic development and lead to new features in species.

The challenge to religious belief and the responses of believers

Revised

Those religious believers who see an Old Earth and organisms developing over a long period of time do not necessarily regard evolution as a challenge to religious belief. What they reject is the idea that the order and apparent design in nature is the result of blind chance. They see evolution as the mechanism which God used to bring about life, including human life. Events are determined by God, though they appear to be by chance. This does raise the problem of the suffering and waste that is created by the evolutionary process. John Polkinghorne, an Anglican priest who also had been a professor of mathematical physics at Cambridge University, argued:

> The actual balance between chance and necessity ... which we perceive, seems to me to be consistent with the will of a patient and subtle Creator, content to achieve his purposes through the unfolding of process and accepting thereby a measure of the vulnerability and precariousness which always characterise the gift of freedom by love.

God designed a system whereby law and chance could lead to life and mind and the diverse dimensions of human experience.

The Catholic Church

The Catholic Church argues that human beings are unique and spiritual on the grounds that God infuses souls into human beings, regardless of what process God might have used to create our physical bodies. More recently, in July 2007, Pope Benedict XVI said that there is strong scientific evidence for the theory of evolution, but the theory does not answer the question 'From where does everything come?'

A false theory

Other religious believers see evolution as totally denying God and so reject evolution as a false theory. They point out flaws in the theory, such as the absence of transitional forms in the fossil record. They regard the religious texts as revelations from God and the source of truth.

Issues arising

One of the major issues arising is the relationship between science and religion. To what extent are they in conflict?

Typical mistake

Candidates often learn quotes but mistakenly think that a quote without a comment will suffice as an explanation. The quote should exemplify the point rather than stand alone as an explanation in itself.

Key quote

'After Darwin we are bound in the end to be committed to a non-dualistic view of both human beings and the world.'

(Don Cupitt)

Now test yourself

8 Explain what is meant by the term 'survival of the fittest' as used in evolution.

9 How might a religious believer reply to the challenge that evolution shows that events are blind chance?

Answers online

Tested

Science and religion – conflicted, complementary or irrelevant?

Areas of potential conflict between science and religion

- 'God is an unnecessary **hypothesis**. All things can be explained naturally' versus 'Scientific methodology cannot explain everything'.

- 'Scientific method is the only reliable way to knowledge' versus 'Knowledge from God is by revelation'.

- 'Scientific theories and concepts provide a full account of reality' versus 'Reality consists of more than just the material'.

- 'Science accepts only the material' versus 'Religion accepts the supernatural'.

> **Hypothesis** – a suggested explanation.

Areas where science and religion probably complement each other

- The theories of the Big Bang and evolution do not necessarily deny the existence of God.

- God may be revealed both in nature and in scripture.

- Both science and religion believe in the use of reason.

- Both science and religion presuppose many things that must be taken on faith.

- Many scientists are religious believers.

> **Key quote**
>
> 'It is often said that science cannot prove the existence of God. Yet science does have value in theological debate because it gives us new concepts that sometimes make popular notions of God untenable.'
>
> (Paul Davies)

Areas where science and religion are possibly irrelevant to each other

- Science is trying to answer the 'how' questions whereas religion is trying to answer the 'why' questions.

- Science is based totally on human observation and reason. Religion is based partly on divine revelation.

- Science tends to be impersonal but religion tends to be concerned with the personal.

> **Exam tip**
>
> Do not feel that you must reach a conclusion. Not being able to reach a conclusion is an acceptable answer. However, there has to be justification in your answer as to why no one particular conclusion can be fully supported.

> **God of the gaps** – gaps in scientific knowledge are taken to be evidence or proof of God's existence.

Implications for religion of the idea of God as an explanation for the unexplained

Science has unanswered questions – things that, as yet, have not been explained. Sometimes, religious believers argue that if science cannot explain how something happened, then God must be the explanation. Such arguments are called '**God of the gaps**' arguments. Clearly this approach has a number of problems:

> **Exam tip**
>
> Be careful when using quotes in critical assessments. Make sure that they relate to the argument that is presented. To make sure of this, always explain the relevance of the quote in your answer.

- As the frontiers of knowledge are being pushed further and further back, then God is being pushed back with them, and is therefore continually in retreat.

- Religious believers think God is more than a 'God of the gaps'. Some believe God is always at work in the natural world, in the gaps as well as in the areas that science can explain. God is not hiding in the recesses of the unknown or excluded from the rest of nature.

- For many religious believers, the more they understand the workings of the universe then the more they see evidence of God.

- In 1944, a German theologian named Dietrich Bonhoeffer wrote: 'We are to find God in what we know, not in what we don't know; God wants us to realise his presence, not in unsolved problems but in those that are solved.'

- If the evidence for believing in God rests on a 'God of the gaps' argument, then as science provides an explanation, belief in God diminishes.

Strengths and weaknesses of religious responses to challenges posed by scientific views

Revised

This issue requires you to weigh up how strong or weak the responses are to the challenges posed by scientific views. The various challenges and responses can be found on pages 121–129. This means discussing how persuasive they are, rather than just stating what the responses are.

Take, for example, the response that argues that God was the cause of the start of the Big Bang. Some may argue that this is a weak attempt to make the existence of God consistent with the theory of the start of the universe. It is weak because there may be other explanations of what led to the Big Bang, such as the following:

● The Big Bang is the result of a Big Crunch and an endless cycle of such sequences.

● Some scientists think that string theory may provide an answer, together with the theory that there are possibly an infinite number of universes.

● Others look for an explanation in quantum physics and the uncertainty principle. These theories may support the idea of a spontaneous creation of particles.

● Yet others point out that God is a weak answer since it explains nothing. If God has no cause then why does the universe have to have a cause?

Remember that weighing up involves evaluation and not just reciting the arguments.

Intelligent design – scientific or religious theory?

Revised

The theory of intelligent design holds that certain features of the universe and of living things are best explained by an intelligent cause, not an undirected process such as natural selection. Supporters of intelligent design argue that it is different from creationism because it starts with the empirical evidence of nature and seeks to ascertain what inferences can be drawn from that evidence. It does not start from religious texts nor does it claim that an intelligent cause could be supernatural.

Intelligent design *is* scientific	Intelligent design is *not* scientific
The scientific method is commonly described as a four-step process involving observations, hypothesis, experiments and conclusion. Intelligent design claims to follow this methodology.	Intelligent design might base its ideas on observations in the natural world, but it does not test them in the natural world, or attempt to develop mechanisms (such as natural selection) to explain its observations.
Intelligent design theory can say nothing about the designer other than that the designer was intelligent.	It does not consider alternative explanations for irreducibly complex systems. It claims irreducibly complex systems cannot be produced through natural selection.
It does not claim evolution cannot produce irreducibly complex systems – only that it is empirically implausible.	Many regard intelligent design as more a religious theory. It offers no testable hypothesis and so must be taken on faith.
Although it rejects the theory of natural selection as a sufficient explanation for the evolving of species, it does usually accept an intelligence-driven form of evolutionary process.	

Now test yourself

Tested

10 Explain what is meant by the phrase 'God of the gaps'.

11 Explain three areas where science and religion are possibly irrelevant to each other.

Answers online

Exam practice

(a) Explain the 'Big Bang' theory. (30 marks)

(b) To what extent do scientific views of the orgin of the universe leave no room for God? (15 marks)

Answers online

Online

4.3 The design argument

Forms of the argument

There are a variety of forms of the design argument. Only those listed in the exam specifications are discussed below. All the arguments are **inductive** and **a posteriori**.

> **Inductive** – a process of reasoning that draws a general conclusion from specific instances. Inductive arguments offer only probabilities, not proofs.
>
> **A posteriori** – after experience, derived from observed facts.

Aquinas — Revised ☐

The philosopher and theologian Thomas Aquinas (1225–74) wrote a compact form of the arguments for the existence of God and these have become known as the Five Ways. It is the Fifth Way that deals with the design argument:

1 There are things without knowledge that act for an end. (An 'end' is the goal towards which a thing moves. Aquinas used the example of an acorn whose end was an oak tree.)

2 If something without knowledge acts for an end, then it must be because it is directed by a being with knowledge and intelligence.

3 Therefore, there must be an intelligent being by whom all natural things are directed to their end.

4 This being we call God.

5 Just as an archer (intelligent being) must direct an arrow (an object without knowledge), God must direct nature.

> **Typical mistake**
>
> Candidates often begin their account of Aquinas' argument with a lengthy paragraph recounting irrelevant biographical details and/or listing all of his Five Ways. Marks are awarded for the demonstration of an understanding of the arguments, not for potted biographies.

> **Exam tip**
>
> If no particular form of the design argument is specifically named in the question, then other forms of the design argument, not listed here, can be used (for example, the anthropic argument).

Paley — Revised ☐

William Paley's design arguments were first published in 1802. They reflect the seventeenth-century thinking that viewed the universe as a machine. Although his analogy of the watch was not original, through Paley it became well known.

> **Case study** **Paley's watch**
>
> Suppose you were crossing a heath and came across a watch. Paley argued that, even if you had never seen a watch before, you would know that this instrument did not happen by chance but must be the product of an intelligent mind. All the parts fit together and achieve the purpose of telling the time. The watch must have had an intelligent and skilled maker, who designed it to do what it does. The watch demands a watchmaker and no entirely naturalistic explanation would be acceptable. Likewise, the way the universe fits together, for a purpose, demands an intelligent designer. The designer would have to be God.

Design qua purpose

- The feature of a manufactured machine is that the parts fit together to achieve a specific function (for example, a watch).
- Manufactured machines are the result of intelligent design.
- Objects in nature (for example, the eye – where the parts fit together to achieve the particular purpose of seeing) are **analogous** to manufactured machines.
- Analogous effects have analogous causes.
- Therefore, objects in nature are the result of something analogous to intelligent design.
- The agent responsible for such design must be God.

Paley was aware of criticisms made against his argument and offset them by claiming that the argument was not weakened if:

- we found that the mechanism did not always work perfectly (i.e. the natural world may not always function perfectly)
- there are parts of the machine whose function we do not understand (i.e. we may not understand the purpose of everything in the natural world).

Design qua regularity

Paley also argued that the regularity observed in the universe demanded an intelligent mind as explanation. He used scientific findings from his own time as evidence, such as the way planets obey laws in their movement. The whole universe, and all its parts, seem ordered and act in a regular and predictable way. According to Paley, the agent responsible for such order and regularity must be God.

> **Qua** – a Latin word meaning 'as relating to'.
>
> **Analogous** – a comparison of two or more things to show how they are similar.

> **Exam tip**
>
> If you are asked about Paley's argument, do not just narrate the story of the watch found on the heath. You need to draw out the actual argument from the account. Explain the analogy and what it is implying. This demonstrates knowledge and understanding, through the use of evidence and examples (level 5).

> **Now test yourself**
>
> 1 Explain how Aquinas' example of an archer and an arrow illustrates his argument for the existence of God.
>
> 2 Explain how Paley's example of the watch illustrates his argument for the existence of God.
>
> **Answers online**
>
> Tested ☐

Swinburne

Revised ☐

The philosopher Richard Swinburne (b. 1934) offers different forms of the design argument, including '**spatial order**' and '**temporal order**'.

Spatial order

In the spatial order argument, Swinburne reformulates Paley's argument:

- Swinburne's reason for reformulation is that the theory of evolution by **natural selection** provides an adequate explanation for complex animals and plants, without any need to appeal to the existence of God.
- Instead of Paley's analogy between objects in nature and manufactured machines, Swinburne's analogy is between nature, as a machine that produces other machines such as animals, and a machine-making machine made by human beings (for example, a robot in a car factory).
- By analogy, just as human beings (as rational agents) are responsible for man-made machines, so God (as a rational agent) is responsible for nature.
- Swinburne regards the universe as being fine-tuned for life by this rational agent (for example, if the physical fundamental constants, such as the gravitational constant or the speed of light, had been slightly different, life would have been impossible in the universe).
- Swinburne acknowledges that the argument from spatial order is not very strong.

> **Spatial order** – the arrangement of things (for example, the complex structures of organisms such as plants and animals).
>
> **Temporal order** – patterns of behaviour of objects, such as their behaviour in accordance with the laws of nature.
>
> **Natural selection** – a key mechanism of evolution. It is the principle by which each slight variation, if useful, is preserved and the trait passed on to the next generation.

Exam practice answers at **www.therevisionbutton.co.uk/myrevisionnotes**

Temporal order

In the temporal order argument, Swinburne argues as follows:

- The universe is orderly, yet it could have been chaotic.

- Nature appears to have laws which are constant (for example, the law of gravity).

- If there is an explanation for an orderly universe, then the explanation cannot be a scientific one. This is because science tells us these laws exist but it does not tell us *why* they exist – why there is order rather than chaos.

- Therefore, if the order of the universe is to be explained, it must be in terms of the purposes of an intelligent being.

- Such a being must be of infinite power and knowledge; i.e. God.

Key quote

'So either the orderliness of nature is where all explanation stops, or we must postulate an agent of such great power and knowledge … the simplest such agent … God.'
(Richard Swinburne)

Now test yourself

3 According to Swinburne, what is the difference between spatial order and temporal order?

4 Why did Swinburne need to reformulate Paley's argument?

Answers online

Tested

Key criticisms of the design argument

From philosophy, with reference to David Hume — Revised

Paley's argument was published 26 years after the death of philosopher David Hume (1711–76). However, Hume had strongly attacked a similar form of the design argument to the one that Paley later used. Hume's main arguments against the design qua purpose are set out below.

An unsound analogy

- Our world is not like a machine, since it is composed of vegetables and animals. It is more organic than it is mechanical. The world would be better compared to a carrot.

- Intelligence is not the necessary governing principle behind the world. There could be many governing principles: for example, reproduction in animals and gravity in the movements of planets.

Similar effects do not necessarily imply similar causes

- Different causes can result in the same effect (for example, different medicines can produce the same healing).

- To know that an orderly universe must arise from intelligence and thought, we would have to have experienced the origin of the world.

The analogy makes God more human than divine

- The more you press the analogy of the manufactured machine (for example, a watch) with the universe, the more human you have to make God, since similar effects imply similar causes.

- We cannot ascribe infinity to God because the cause ought only to be proportional to the effect, but the universe is not infinite.

Typical mistake

Candidates often wrongly claim that Hume was criticising Paley's argument. Paley wrote his design argument *after* Hume had written his challenges. Hume never read Paley's work. Paley's argument using analogy was not original to Paley; Paley merely popularised it.

- Because the universe contains imperfections, we cannot ascribe to God perfection. Also, many worlds might have been botched and bungled before this universe was made.
- A number of people might be involved in designing a machine – so a committee of gods may be involved in design of the universe.

The analogy leads to a non-moral God
- Unpleasant features of nature, such as earthquakes and disease, suggest the planning and design could not be that of a just and good God.
- There could be two forces, one good and one evil.

Other explanations for apparent order
- The universe could be the result of some blind cosmic accident (for example, the **Epicurean hypothesis**).
- The universe is bound to have the appearance of design, since there could be no universe at all if the parts of it were not mutually adapted to some degree.
- It is not surprising we find order. Unless the universe was an orderly place, people would not be around to comment on its existence.

> **Epicurean hypothesis** – given enough time, even in a random chaotic universe, order would still develop.

Key quote

> 'Nearly all the things which men are hanged or imprisoned for doing to one another are nature's everyday performances.'
>
> (John Stuart Mill)

From science, with reference to Richard Dawkins

Revised

Naturalistic explanation

Charles Darwin (1809–82) demonstrated that order was not necessarily evidence of purpose and design. Order could result from blind chance. The theory of evolution suggests that the combination of variation and survival leads eventually to the emergence of organisms that are suited to their environment. They will have the appearance of design but will be the result of evolving by variation and survival.

Scientist Richard Dawkins (b. 1941) attacked Paley's argument by pointing out that a true watchmaker has foresight. He designs his cogs and springs and has a future purpose in mind. In contrast, natural selection is blind, unconscious and an automatic process. It is a blind watchmaker and God is an unnecessary hypothesis.

Memes

According to Dawkins, the Darwinian approach also applies to culture. **Memes** are similar to ideas, or culture, that spread from person to person. A meme acts as a unit for carrying cultural ideas, symbols or practices, which can be transmitted from one mind to another through such means as writing, speech, gestures, rituals. They operate by natural selection. Just as genes propagate themselves in the gene pool by leaping from body to body via sperm and eggs, so memes propagate themselves in the meme pool by leaping from brain to brain by a process broadly called imitation.

Dawkins argues that memes can account for people's belief in God. The 'god-meme' is like a virus that spreads the idea of God into cultures.

Key quote

> 'The only watchmaker in nature is the blind forces of physics.'
>
> (Richard Dawkins)

Key quote

> 'Belief in God is to be seen as "self-replicating information".'
>
> (Richard Dawkins)

> **Meme** – a memory or idea that is inherited; a term invented by Dawkins to refer to a unit of cultural inheritance.

Now test yourself

5 Explain how Hume's suggestion that the world is better compared to a carrot challenges one form of the design argument.

6 How does the theory of evolution challenge the design argument?

Answers online

Tested

Responses to these arguments

Challenges from philosophy	Responses
An unsound analogy.	Both nature and the watch display purpose. Purpose shouts for an explanation.
	Vegetables show features of design.
Similar effects do not necessarily imply similar causes.	Order and purpose are usually created by intelligence. There would need to be good reason why an alternative should be considered.
The analogy makes God more human than divine.	Analogies, by their very nature, usually make one telling point. The pictures they use cannot be interpreted rigidly in every detail.
	The idea that the analogy leads to supposing a whole community of gods can be challenged on the basis of **Ockham's razor**.
The analogy leads to a non-moral God.	The design argument is part of a cumulative argument and does not claim to demonstrate all the attributes of God in each argument.
	Philosophy has **theodicies** that address the problem of evil.
Unless the universe was an orderly place, people would not be around to comment on its existence.	The existence of an observer has no bearing on the probability of the occurrence of the events being observed. What needs explaining is the occurrence of the event, not the fact that I can view the event. (Swinburne uses his story of the card-shuffling machine to illustrate this – see below.)

Challenges from science	Responses
Evolution	Science can neither prove nor disprove the existence of God.
	Darwinism is compatible with conventional religious beliefs and with atheism.
Memes	There is no direct observational evidence for the existence of 'memes'.
	Is there an 'atheism-meme'?
	Ideas are abstract; they are not physical objects.

Ockham's razor – the principle states that entities should not be multiplied beyond necessity. The name derives from the idea of 'shaving off' those entities that are not needed.

Theodicy – a justification of the righteousness of God, given the existence of evil.

Key quote

'The teleologist's starting point is not that we perceive order rather than disorder, but that order rather than disorder is there.'

(Richard Swinburne)

Key quote

'… if memes really existed they would ultimately deny the reality of reflective thought.'

(Anthony O'Hear)

Key quote

'… we don't know what memes are made of, or where they reside.'

(Susan Blackmore)

Now test yourself

7 Explain Swinburne's card-shuffling machine illustration.

Answer online

Case study Swinburne's card-shuffling machine illustration

Suppose that a madman kidnaps a victim and shuts him in a room with a card-shuffling machine. The machine shuffles ten decks of cards simultaneously and then draws a card from each deck and exhibits simultaneously the ten cards. The kidnapper tells the victim that he will shortly set the machine to work and it will exhibit its first draw, but that unless the draw consists of an ace of hearts from each deck, the machine will simultaneously set off an explosion which will kill the victim, in consequence of which he will not see which cards the machine drew.

The machine is then set to work, and to the amazement and relief of the victim the machine exhibits an ace of hearts drawn from each deck. The victim thinks that this extraordinary fact needs an explanation in terms of the machine having been rigged in some way. But the kidnapper, who now reappears, casts doubt on this suggestion. 'It is hardly surprising', he says, 'that the machine draws only aces of hearts. You could not possibly see anything else. For you would not be here to see anything at all, if any other cards had been drawn.'

Issues arising

Strengths and weaknesses of the design argument

Revised

Strengths	Weaknesses
Science shows how finely tuned the universe is, which is conducive to our survival.	It offers inductive arguments – probability not a proof.
It is consistent with God as the explanation of a complex universe.	The theory of evolution gives a non-supernatural explanation.
Criticisms of it fail.	Criticisms of it are persuasive.
It is part of the **cumulative argument for God**.	

Cumulative argument for God
– arguments for the existence of God that do not consist of a single decisive argument and none of which has decisive force, but the cumulative case is alleged to make the existence of God probable.

Exam tip

Addressing issues arising is an AO2 skill and therefore is *not* about listing strengths and weaknesses. Rather it involves discussing the relative weightings of the strengths against the weaknesses. AO2 always involves some evaluating.

How far does the design argument make it reasonable to believe in God?

Revised

Here is a series of questions that you should be asking yourself as you get your head round this issue:

- What counts as 'reasonable'?
- Does Swinburne's argument successfully deal with the challenge from the theory of evolution?
- Which is a more reasonable explanation of the universe – that it is a blind cosmic accident or that there is an intelligence designing it? How do you decide?
- Is the assumption that similar effects imply similar causes a valid one?
- How convincing are the criticisms of the design argument?
- Is 'God' the only conclusion?

How far has Swinburne's argument successfully met the challenges of philosophy and science?

Revised

This issue requires a weighing-up of the success, or failure, of the above arguments and responses. Ask yourself some key questions about the challenges to Swinburne's design argument, for example:

- Is Swinburne's card-shuffling illustration an effective response to the challenge from philosophy?
- How much of a threat to the design argument is the theory of evolution?
- Does Swinburne's acceptance of the theory of evolution seriously weaken his argument?

Now test yourself   Tested

8   'God is the only solution that explains the order and purpose in the universe.' Justify this claim and then challenge this claim.

9   List three points to support the view that the design argument successfully meets the challenge of philosophy.

Answers online

Exam practice

(a) Explain Paley's design argument for the existence of God.   (30 marks)

(b) 'Paley's design argument for the existence of God has more weaknesses than strengths.' To what extent do you agree?   (15 marks)

Answers online

Online

4.4 Quantum mechanics and a religious world view

Challenges to Newtonian physics

Prior to **quantum theory**, the scientific view of the universe was shaped by **Newtonian physics**.

Newtonian physics Revised

Quantum theory challenges three previously held Newtonian ideas.

1 Newtonian physics provides a realistic description of the universe

This means:

- it describes the universe as it is in itself, distinct from the observer
- such things as mass and velocity are considered objective realities of the universe
- every event takes place in space and time, and is independent of the observer.

> **Quantum theory** – a theory that describes the behaviour of subatomic particles.
>
> **Newtonian physics** – the world view underlying traditional science based on Newton's law of mechanics; sometimes referred to as 'mechanistic'.

2 Newtonian physics is deterministic

This means:

- the movement of matter is predictable
- given a body's present state, it is possible to calculate its future path and to reconstruct any earlier state that it has gone through
- laws seem to govern everything from particles to planets
- nature is a law-abiding machine.

3 Newtonian physics outlook is reductionistic

This means:

- if the behaviour of the smallest parts that make up the whole can be identified, then the workings of the whole can also be explained
- the parts that make up the whole, though they are rearranged, do not themselves change.

> **Deterministic** – not random.
>
> **Reductionistic** – the analysis of complex things into less complex constituents.

How quantum theory challenges the views of Newtonian physics Revised

Quantum theory developed when the Newtonian approach failed to explain some observations; for example, why certain objects changed colour when heated. The challenge posed by quantum theory to this

Newtonian view is so great that the scientist Thomas Kuhn referred to it as a **paradigm shift**.

The changes to Newtonian physics that quantum theory suggests are as follows:

1 In the Newtonian view, the atom is pictured as electrons orbiting around a nucleus. Although unobservable, the model is seen as a realistic description of nature. Quantum theory undermines this idea because it claims it is not possible to describe the behaviour of **subatomic particles** so precisely. In addition, in quantum theory, the observer is always a participant.

2 In the Newtonian view, nature obeys laws and is predictable. Physicists prefer to describe quantum effects using probability. It is not a lack of knowledge that makes nature difficult to predict. Unpredictability is in the nature of matter itself.

3 In the Newtonian view, protons, neutrons and electrons are indivisible basic building blocks of matter. In quantum theory, other types of particles have been identified and all are now thought to be composed of even smaller particles called quarks. When they combine to make new protons and particles they exhibit new properties and activities not found in their components.

> **Paradigm shift** – a radical change from one way of thinking to another way of thinking.
>
> **Subatomic particles** – particles smaller than an atom such as quarks, leptons and Higgs boson.

> **Now test yourself**
>
> 1 What three previously held Newtonian ideas does quantum mechanics challenge?
>
> 2 How does quantum mechanics challenge these three ideas?
>
> **Answers online**
>
> Tested ☐

Key ideas in the world view of quantum mechanics

Quanta ——————————————————————— Revised ☐

'Quanta' is the plural of 'quantum' and means a small but definite amount. In quantum mechanics, quanta are packets of energy at the subatomic level, changing the idea that the atom was the smallest bit of reality. It is the minimum amount of any physical entity involved in an interaction. The fact that energy can come in the form of little packets rather than just in **waves** was a discovery that changed the way scientists viewed the behaviour of matter in the universe.

> **Wave** – a disturbance in some type of substance, like ripples through water.

Light as a wave and a particle ———————————— Revised ☐

In the seventeenth and eighteenth centuries, light had been understood as small discrete **particles** which travelled in a straight line. This was because light always seemed to travel in straight beams rather than in a ripple-spreading path like a wave.

> **Particle** – what we perceive as matter, something with mass.

The two-slit experiment

In the early 1800s an English scientist, Thomas Young, demonstrated that light was a wave. Young shone a form of light in a straight line through two slits and allowed the light to strike a screen on the other side. The expectation was that it would show a pattern corresponding to the size and shape of the two slits.

This is the pattern that particles would give. However, when Young performed the experiment he found that a diffraction pattern appeared on the screen. A diffraction pattern is characteristic of wave motion. It seemed clear that light was not particles but a wave.

Light as a particle

In 1905, physicist Albert Einstein showed that the explanation of certain phenomena was that light is composed of discrete quanta, called photons, rather than continuous waves. In other words, light behaves as if it were a particle. This meant there were two conflicting theories. Is light composed of particles or waves?

Wave–particle duality

In the early 1920s, the French physicist Louis de Broglie looked at the problem in a reverse way. He investigated whether atoms were particles or waves. His theoretical work suggested that all quantum entities share a wave–particle duality. However, at this stage it was still only a theory.

Eventually technology made it possible to conduct the two-slit experiment with individual particles. It was found that sending particles through a two-slit apparatus one at a time resulted in single particles appearing on the screen. However, an interference pattern emerges when these particles are allowed to build up one by one. This suggests that each electron was interfering with itself, and therefore in some sense the electron had to be going through both slits at once. This idea contradicts our everyday experience of discrete objects. Matter (electrons) and energy (photons) both exhibit wave–particle duality, but they cannot be both a wave and a particle at the same time.

The nature of the electron
Revised

The two-slit apparatus was then modified by adding particle detectors positioned at the slits. This enabled the experimenter to find the position of a particle when it passed through the two-slit apparatus. It was hoped that this experiment would show whether it went through only one of the slits, as a particle would be expected to do, or through both, as a wave would be expected to do.

However, the results were surprising. It seems that it depends on which experiment is being performed as to whether the electron behaves as a wave or a particle. The observation of the electrons seems to influence the outcome. The observer is not a mere spectator but becomes an actor, affecting what is happening.

More recent variations of the two-slit experiment include the particle detectors showing which path the electron took only after it has passed through the slit. In this case, it seems that observing the electron at this stage can retroactively alter its previous behaviour at the slits.

Therefore, the way that the electron is viewed is intimately linked with the way it is measured, and certain experiments will determine how the electron behaves.

Typical mistake

A common mistake is to list the various experiments but not explain the significance of them and how they contributed to the development of quantum theory.

Now test yourself

3 Explain how the two-slit experiment showed light to be a wave.

4 Explain what is meant by 'wave–particle duality'.

Answers online

Tested

Exam tip

This section is full of new concepts. In your revision, instead of just drawing up a glossary of key words, try changing this into a flowchart that links each aspect of the topic together. This will help to demonstrate 'good understanding' of the topic overall (AO1).

The electron undermines the Newtonian world view

Being uncertain about how to picture the electron undermines all three aspects of the Newtonian world view:

- Science cannot have a 'real' picture of the electron as a particle because the electron is not always a particle.
- Since the electron appears to behave in different, contradictory ways, it is not possible to be certain about it. This lack of certainty undermines the principle of determinism.
- Scientific reductionism of the kind envisaged by the Newtonian world view is only possible if the behaviour of the constituent parts is predictable. As explained above, the behaviour of subatomic particles like the electron is not precisely predictable, which suggests that reductionism is thereby undermined.

Key quote

'Do not keep saying to yourself, if you can possibly avoid it, "But how can it be like that?" because you will go … into a blind alley from which nobody has escaped. Nobody knows how it can be like that.'

(American theoretical physicist Richard Feynman, speaking about a quantum entity such as a photon)

Now test yourself

5 Explain how the modern view of the electron undermines the principle of determinism.

Answer online

Tested ☐

The role of the observer in resolving uncertainty

Revised ☐

In 1927 the German theoretical physicist and philosopher Werner Heisenberg calculated that it is possible to measure the position of an electron and its momentum but you cannot measure precisely both at the same time. The more precisely you measure one of the properties, the less precisely you are able to measure the other property. This understanding became known as the Uncertainty Principle.

Key quote

'The more precisely the position is determined, the less precisely the momentum is known in this instant, and vice versa.'

(Werner Heisenberg)

Implications for the nature of reality

Revised ☐

There are a number of interpretations of quantum mechanics – some of which are listed below:

- Albert Einstein believed that quantum mechanics would be seen to be deterministic. It was just a lack of present knowledge rather than matter being unpredictable. Hence his famous quote that 'God does not play dice with the Universe'.

- Others conclude that there will always be some uncertainty about these particles. The uncertainty will not be the result of a failing in human knowledge. Neither will the uncertainty be the consequence of unsophisticated methods of measurement. The uncertainty is real – objectively there.

- The Danish physicist, Niels Bohr, proposed the Copenhagen interpretation of quantum theory. He argued that an electron is both a wave and a particle until the act of experimental measurement or some other interaction. This interaction forces it to be one or the other. Bohr argued that the very act of measurement affects what we observe. The scientist can no longer stand apart from the process of the experiment but must accept that his or her involvement will shape the outcome of the experiment itself. Serious questions are then raised about what is objectively real. This understanding of matter appears to do away with the concept of a reality separate from one's observations.

Typical mistake

Do not make the mistake of simply describing what each scientist has said. Note the focus of the question and select your material that specifically addresses that focus.

Exam practice answers at **www.therevisionbutton.co.uk/myrevisionnotes**

- An Austrian physicist named Erwin Schrödinger did not agree with the Copenhagen interpretation. He sought to challenge it by using an illustration. He was trying to show that what was being claimed about the nature and behaviour of subatomic particles was wrong. His approach was to take Bohr's idea and then apply it to large-scale system in order to critique Bohr's view. Schrödinger's illustration involved a steel box, a cat, a test tube of hydrocyanic acid and a small amount of a radioactive substance. As the radioactive substance decays, a single atom will trigger a mechanism to open the poison and kill the cat. It is not possible to know when the atom triggers the release of the poison. So it is not possible to calculate when the cat will be killed. Until the box is opened the cat is both dead and alive. Schrödinger is pointing out how absurd this is, yet that is similar to what the Copenhagen interpretation is saying in regard to electrons.

- Another interpretation of quantum theory is the many-worlds interpretation, proposed by the American physicist Hugh Everett. Instead of reality being viewed as a single unfolding history, the many-worlds interpretation views reality as a many-branched tree, wherein every possible quantum outcome is realised. This view claims to reconcile the observation of unpredictability with the fully deterministic equations of quantum mechanics. It explains that quantum objects display several behaviours because they inhabit an infinite number of parallel universes.

Key quote

'Everything we call real is made of things that cannot be regarded as real.'

(Niels Bohr)

Exam tip

It is important that you associate the correct scientist with the correct theory. Quotes can be useful but it is more important that you are able to understand and explain their ideas.

Now test yourself

6 How did Einstein's view of quantum mechanics differ from that of Bohr's view?

7 Explain how Schrödinger's illustration about the cat in the box challenges the Copenhagen interpretation of quantum mechanics.

Answers online

Tested ☐

Quantum mechanics and religion

Parallels with mystical insights into the nature of reality

Revised ☐

There have been a number of books written that draw parallels between quantum mechanics and Eastern mysticism. One of the most influential is Fritjof Capra's *The Tao of Physics* (1977).

Key feature	Found in quantum mechanics	Found in mysticism
Difficulty of description	Paradoxes such as wave–particle duality make it difficult to describe what happens at the subatomic level.	A key characteristic of mystical experiences is ineffability – i.e. the experience is incapable of being described in words.
Duality	Subatomic particles appear to behave like waves and like particles. Reality appears to consist of mutually contradictory yet mutually dependent states.	In Chinese Taoism, duality is represented by the powerful concept of Yin/Yang.
Sense of underlying unity in reality	Quantum mechanics points to the unity and interconnectedness of all events.	Eastern mysticism presents unity of all things. There is one ultimate reality – Brahman – with which the individual is merged. Western mystical traditions also talk about **absorption**, e.g. Theresa of Avila. Both **extrovertive** and **introvertive** types of mysticism have the characteristic of unity of all things.

Key feature	Found in quantum mechanics	Found in mysticism
The world is dynamic and ever-changing.	Matter appears as energy, and energy appears as matter. Particles are continually being created and destroyed.	All life is transitory. All existence is impermanent.
Human knowledge is **contingent** and limited.	In the quantum world there is no exact fit for reality.	Mystics acknowledge the limits of human knowledge when they speak about the numinous (see page 89).
The effect of the observer on what is observed.	The mind plays an important role in the construction of reality. Quantum variables have no definite values until they are observed.	The mystic receives knowledge through personal involvement with God. The mystic gives a subjective interpretation of ultimate reality.

Some, such as Ian Barbour (*Religion in an Age of Science*, 1990), argue that Capra has overstated the case for parallels between quantum mechanics and mysticism. See, for example, the following:

1 While mystics speak of the unity of all things, especially in the depth of meditation, the wholeness and unity that physics expresses is highly differentiated and structured, subject to strict restraints, principles and laws.

2 In some mystic traditions, the temporal world is illusory. Quantum mechanics is more about temporal change.

3 The goal of mysticism is to understand ultimate reality. Through meditation, a mystic seeks a new state of consciousness. In contrast, the goal of science is to explain the nature of the world, possibly by means of a new conceptual system.

Absorption – loss of individual personality, losing of the self.

Extrovertive mysticism – the subject 'looks outward through the senses' and grasps the unity of all things.

Introvertive mysticism – the subject 'looks inward into the mind', to achieve 'pure consciousness'.

Contingent – uncertain but possible.

The implications of quantum mechanics for religion

Revised

For some, quantum mechanics has implication for the religious believer:

● Whereas a Newtonian world view assumed that science can explain everything, in a quantum world where there is no exact fit for reality, the possibility of God is not ruled out.

● Quantum mechanics has difficulties with description and this is mirrored in religion.

● Quantum mechanics supports the mystical notion of unity (no subjective/objective divide).

● Quantum mechanics is in tune with the religious idea that human knowledge will always be partial or contingent.

● Quantum mechanics uses models (for example, wave and particle models) to describe what is happening in nature. Religious believers use models (for example, God as king) in religious language to describe God.

● The unpredictability of nature indicated by quantum mechanics allows for the idea of God controlling the world at a subatomic level. This could indicate the involvement of God within creation at all levels.

● The idea that quanta appear without causation challenges the religious notion of an ordered, purposeful creation.

● Some see the beauty of the mathematics involved in quantum mechanics as evidence of God and human free will.

Typical mistake

It is a mistake to think it is sufficient just to learn a list of succinct key points or phrases. Revision points are reminders of key areas and you need to be able to develop them rather than just reciting a list.

Exam tip

It is important to use technical terms where appropriate.

Now test yourself

8 Give three ways in which quantum theory is *not* paralleled to mysticism.

9 Explain the view that the unpredictability of nature indicated by quantum mechanics allows for the idea of God.

Answers online

Tested

Issues arising

How important is 'agreement' with science for religion?

Revised

This depends how literally a religious believer interprets their religious texts. Some may regard religious texts as non-literal and therefore see no conflict with scientific findings. Others may interpret religious texts about the way the world is in a more literal way. The table below considers this more literal approach to the interpretation of religious texts.

Can science and religion agree?

Can make agreement possible	Cannot make agreement possible
Both emphasise the unity of reality. Science reveals universal laws. Religion reveals a universal God.	The religious texts conflict with scientific findings, e.g. about the creation of the universe.
Both acknowledge the limitations of human knowledge. Science – in terms of the physical reality of the universe; religion – in terms of the spiritual reality of God.	Some scientists do not consider their uncertainty as objectively real. It is because of the lack of present knowledge. Given time, science will explain everything.
Both are subject to changes of understanding and views.	Science deals with empirical evidence and testing. Religion accepts **revelation** and the **metaphysical**.
Science answers 'how' questions. Religion answers 'why' questions and considers the purpose of things. Therefore they are not necessarily in disagreement.	Science is about theory. Religion is about faith.
Science can provide evidence to support religious teaching, e.g. the Big Bang caused by God, evolution seen as the work of God.	Quantum mechanics has no connection with the metaphysical.
The orderliness of the universe supports the idea of the existence of God.	The universe can be explained without the need to introduce the idea of a God.

Exam tip

Always make sure that you consider different views in your evaluation.

Revelation – something that is disclosed or communicated by God.

Metaphysical – relating to a reality beyond what is perceptible to the senses.

Now test yourself

10 How would you argue against the view that science and religion agree because they both acknowledge the limitations of human knowledge?

Answer online

Tested

Has science 'discovered' something that mystics knew all along?

Revised

Mystical traditions have been around a great deal longer than quantum mechanics. In this sense, some of the truths of mysticism, such as:

● that reality is unified
● that knowledge is partial and contingent
● that truth can be difficult to describe adequately

have been around long before this was established in quantum mechanics. What the new science does is open up the possibility of a fruitful dialogue between religions with mystical traditions and quantum mechanics. Whereas science and religion are often seen to be at war with each other, now it can be argued that quantum mechanics provides additional support for mystical truths which go back many hundreds of years. It is as though mystics have travelled the path towards truth first and, many years later, scientists have finally caught up.

On the other hand, there is no widespread agreement among scientists about the implications of quantum mechanics:

- The fact that it is difficult to describe quantum effects is significant only in that it demonstrates that language is not adequate. Scientists tend to use mathematics as the preferred method of description of quantum effects and in making this choice they argue there is a great deal of precision. Many religious people also point out that the language of mysticism and the language of quantum mechanics are entirely different from one another.

- There is no claim in mysticism to empirical reality. A mystical experience is often entirely un-empirical. While some interpretations of the significance of quantum mechanics argue that there is no such thing as empirical reality, these are regarded as extreme by the great majority of scientists.

So, it is not the case that scientists are discovering ancient truths which have been known by mystics all along because the entire quantum project is a wholly different thing.

Now test yourself

11 State one argument that supports the view that science has 'discovered' something that mystics have known all along.

12 State one argument that challenges the view that science has 'discovered' something that mystics have known all along.

Answers online

Tested ☐

Can science be religious? ———————————————— Revised ☐

This is a different issue from whether there is agreement between science and religion. The issue as to whether science can be 'religious' focuses on the aspects of science that are deemed also to be religious in their character.

Evaluating the extent to which science can be 'religious'

Science can be 'religious'	Science is not 'religious'
Quantum mechanics reveals a more mysterious world, a world that is difficult to describe. Mystical traditions also refer to the ineffability of religious experiences.	Science uses scientific principles to acquire knowledge. It is about empirical data and can be tested. Religion acquires knowledge through revelation and faith, and is about the metaphysical. Therefore science and religion are about two different ways of dealing with two different things.
Quantum mechanics brings a unity to reality with laws that are universal. Mystical traditions such as extrovertive mysticism reflect the oneness and unity.	Science is not concerned with the personal element.
Both exhibit a leap of faith. Both have theories that cannot be verified.	Religion and science use different languages.
Both are human responses to nature. Both seek explanations for the origin of life and the universe.	Diluting science with religious/mystical concepts undermines it.
Both are about human journeys to find meaning and truth which involve faith and trust.	

Now test yourself

13 Explain two ways in which science can be seen as 'religious'.

14 Explain two ways in which science is not 'religious'.

Answers online

Tested ☐

Exam practice

(a) Explain key ideas in the world view of quantum mechanics. **(30 marks)**

(b) 'Quantum mechanics shows that science and religion are not at war with each other.' Assess this claim. **(15 marks)**

Answers online

Online ☐